One Word From God Can Change Your Formula for Success

Harrison House
Tulsa, Oklahoma

09 08 07 06 05 04 03 02 01 00   10 9 8 7 6 5 4 3 2 1

One Word From God Can Change Your Formula for Success
ISBN 1-57794-197-7   30-0714
Copyright © 2000 by Kenneth Copeland Ministries
Fort Worth, Texas 76192-0001

Published by Harrison House, Inc.
P.O. Box 35035
Tulsa, Oklahoma 74153

Contents

Introduction

One Word From God Can Change Your Life FOREVER!

When the revelation of this statement exploded on the inside of me, it changed the way I think...about everything! I had been praying for several days about a situation that seemed at the time to be overwhelming. I had been confessing the Word of God over it, but that Word had begun to come out of my head and not my heart. I was pushing in my flesh for the circumstance to change. As I made my confession one more time, the Spirit of God seemed to say to me, *Why don't you be quiet?!*

I said, "But Lord, I'm confessing the Word!"

He answered inside me, *I know it. I heard you. Now just be still and be quiet a little while, and let the Word of God settle down in your spirit. Quit trying to make this thing happen. You're not God. You're not going to be the one to make it happen anyway!*

So I stopped. I stopped thinking about that situation and began to get quiet before the Lord. And this phrase came up in my spirit: **"One word from God can change anything."**

So I started saying that. I said it off and on all day. It came easily because it came from God—not from my own thinking.

Every time I was tempted to worry or think of ideas concerning my circumstances, I'd think, *Yes, but one word from God...*

I noticed when I'd say that, **the peace of God** would come on me. It was so calming. As a result, a habit developed in me. People would bring me issues. They'd say, "Well, what about..." And I'd either say aloud or think to myself, **"Yeah, that may be so, but one word from God will change anything."**

It began to be the answer for everything. If I was watching television and the newscaster was telling about a disaster, and the people being interviewed were saying things to the effect of "Oh, what are we going to do? It's all been blown away, burned up or shook up...," I'd say, **"Yeah, but one word from God can change anything."**

It really developed into a strength for me, and it can for you, too. That's why we've put together the *One Word From God* Book Series...there could be just one word in these inspiring articles that can change your level of success forever.

You've been searching, seeking help... and God has the answer. He has the one word that can turn your circumstance around and put you on dry ground. He has the one word that gives you all the wisdom that's in Him. He is your Counselor. He wants you to succeed in all that you do. He wants you to be prosperous and have good success (Joshua 1:8).

God loves you. And He has a word for you. One Word that can change your life FOREVER!

Kenneth Copeland

A Supernatural Success

"This book of the law shall not depart out of thy mouth; but thou shalt meditate therein day and night, that thou mayest observe to do according to all that is written therein: for then thou shalt make thy way prosperous, and then thou shalt have good success."
— JOSHUA 1:8

Gloria Copeland

May I ask you a very direct question? How much do you want to succeed in life?

Don't answer that too quickly. Obviously, no one aims to fail at anything they do. But I've been amazed over the years at the people who have come across the formula for success, only to leave it lying on the table while they stay broke, sick and defeated.

Such people initially think success is easy for those who are gifted with great abilities. When they run into the truth, however, it stops them cold. Because the reality of it is: Real supernatural success is no picnic for anyone. It takes courage. It takes faith.

And it doesn't have anything at all to do with natural ability.

If Joshua were around today, he could tell you just how true that is. When God called him to lead Israel after Moses' death, he faced an overwhelming task. As Moses' successor, Joshua had some big shoes to fill. Several million people were under his command, and he knew if they didn't stay in line with God, His blessing would not be on them. Without God's blessing, they would never be able to take the Promised Land.

Joshua had to succeed. The future of the entire nation was at stake. And succeed he did!

How did he do it? By following God's own formula for success.

If you're wishing God would give you such a formula, wish no more. He has. It's the same one He gave to Joshua and it will work just as well for you as it did for him.

Who's With You?

But Gloria, you don't know me! I've tried and failed with every formula in the book. I just don't have what it takes to succeed.

If that's what you're thinking, you haven't tried the formula in God's Book. With His formula, you don't have to "have what it takes." Look at what God said in Joshua 1:5 and you'll see why: *"There shall not any man be able to stand before thee all the days of thy life: as I was with Moses, so I will be with thee: I will not fail thee, nor forsake thee."*

You may remember that God told Moses something very similar in the book of Exodus when Moses claimed he wasn't qualified to go before Pharaoh and demand Israel's freedom. He felt he was personally inadequate for the task. "Lord, who am I to go and do these things?" he asked.

But God answered, *"Certainly I will be with thee"* (Exodus 3:12). In other words, "It doesn't matter who you are, Moses. It matters Who I am, for I am with you!"

That's the great thing about God's success formula. It's not based on our abilities, it's based on His abilities. We may be inadequate in a dozen different ways, but the One Who is with us is more than enough.

An Act of Courage

Although it's great to know God is hooked up with you, that He never leaves you nor forsakes you, before He can release His power on your behalf, you have to be hooked up with Him in return. The way you do that is by obeying His Word. Joshua 1:7 says: *"Only you be strong, and very courageous, that you may do according to all the law, which Moses My servant commanded you. Turn not from it to the right hand or to the left, that you may prosper wherever you go"* (AMP).

Do you know obeying the Word is an act of courage? It really is, because when you obey the Word and believe God in a situation, you're swimming upstream. You're going against the current of the world.

When most of the people and all the circumstances around you are screaming unbelief in your ears, it takes courage to stand on God's Word and not be moved. But once you make the decision to do it, you'll be ready to activate God's three-part formula for success.

You'll find it spelled out in Joshua 1:8: "[1] *This book of the law shall not depart out of your mouth*, [2] *but you shall meditate on it day and night*, [3] *that you may observe and do according to all that is written in it; for then you shall make your way prosperous, and then you shall deal wisely and have good success"* (AMP).

There they are. Three simple steps directly from the mouth of God. Steps that enabled Joshua to conquer the land of Canaan and bring Israel into its inheritance. Steps that will enable you to live like the conqueror God designed you to be.

Let's look at them one by one.

Success Step 1

"This book of the law shall not depart out of your mouth." That's the first element of supernatural success God gives us in this verse. I like to say it this way: Talk the Word.

When I say talk the Word, I don't mean just every now and then when you're feeling spiritual. I mean continually. In

Deuteronomy 6:7, God said you should talk His Word *"when you sit at home and when you walk along the road, when you lie down and when you get up"* (NIV).

That's pretty much all the time, isn't it? At home, at work, in the grocery store—wherever you are—keep the Word of God in your mouth.

Romans 10:17 tells us that *"faith cometh by hearing, and hearing by the word of God."* So when you're continually talking about what God says, what He'll do and what His promises are, you're going to be growing in faith because you're hearing the Word from yourself all the time.

Some people find it hard to talk the Word that much. They just can't seem to do it! If you're one of them, let me tell you why that is.

Jesus said that out of the abundance of the heart the mouth speaketh (Luke 6:45). If you're focusing most of your attention on natural things—watching secular television, going to the movies, thinking about worldly matters, worrying about your job and family—then that's what is going to be in your heart in abundance. And that's what you're going to talk about.

To change what's coming out your mouth, you must refocus your attention. Turn it toward God's Word and keep it there. Fill your heart with an abundance of the Word, and your mouth will get in line.

Success Step 2

That brings us to the second step of God's success formula. *"You shall meditate on it [the Word] day and night"* (AMP).

When you meditate God's Word, you're going to do more than just read it. You're going to take it into your heart in a very personal way and apply it to your own situation.

When you read a scripture about the blessing of prosperity, for example, you won't think, *Hey, that sounds nice, but I could never have it.* Instead, you'll apply it to yourself and say, "Hallelujah! That's God's Word to me. He says He'll meet my needs liberally according to His riches in glory by Christ Jesus, and I'm expecting Him to do that in my situation!"

If you've been reading the Bible like a history book, make a change and begin to see it as God talking directly to you. Take time to meditate on it. Think about it. Digest it. Take it so personally that it moves from your head to your heart, and it will become powerful and active in your life.

Success Step 3

The final step of God's success formula involves action. We must act as though the Word we've been talking and meditating is true—even when circumstances seem to say otherwise.

If that puzzles you, read what Jesus said in Mark 11:

> Have faith in God. For verily I say unto you, That whosoever shall say unto this mountain, Be thou removed, and be thou cast into the sea; and shall not doubt in his heart, but shall believe that those things

**which he saith shall come to pass;
he shall have whatsoever he saith.
Therefore I say unto you, What things
soever ye desire, when ye pray, believe
that ye receive them, and ye shall have
them (verses 22-24).**

Notice Jesus didn't say we should believe
we've received what we ask for when we
see it. He said to believe you receive when
you pray.

Now, if you follow His instructions,
how do you think you're going to act? Are
you going to walk around all depressed and
joyless? Are you going to stand around
wringing your hands worrying?

No! You're going to rejoice and praise
God for the answer to your prayer. You're
going to act like you've already received it.

Right here is where many people miss
it. They know God's Word works, but they
fail to act on it.

You may have been studying the Word for
20 years. You may know how to live by faith
better than anyone around. But, remember, it's

not what you know that will bring you through in victory—it's what you do.

You can walk in faith consistently through 10 trials that come your way and experience great success. Yet on the 11th one, if you neglect to act on the Word, you'll fail. Although the string of victories in your past is a wonderful thing, it's what you do today that will get you through today's test or trial.

More Than Mental Assent

One of the greatest enemies of real faith is a thing I call mental assent. People who operate in mental assent read the Word and think they believe it, but when pressure comes, they don't act on it.

Mental assenters say, "I believe the Bible from cover to cover. I believe I'm healed by the stripes of Jesus because the Bible says so."

But when sickness actually comes and attacks their bodies, they stop saying, "By His stripes I'm healed," and start saying, "I'm sick."

Real faith believes what the Word says even though your eyes and your feelings tell you something different. Faith doesn't care what the symptoms are. It doesn't care what the circumstances look like. It's not moved by what the banker or the doctor or the lawyer or the bill collector says.

Faith in God's Word will change the symptoms. It will change the bank. It will bring the money to get the bills paid. Faith will turn every defeat into victory. It is God's success formula!

But you have to give that faith an opportunity to work. You have to keep God's Word in your mouth and meditate on it in your heart *"that you may observe and do according to all that is written in it; for then you shall make your way prosperous, and then you shall deal wisely and have good success"* (AMP).

No Sorrow Included

Now, think again about that question I asked you earlier. How much do you want to succeed in life? Enough to change what you're saying? Enough to change where your attention is focused? Enough to act on the Word of God even when the rest of the world is telling you it will never work?

If you want it that much, the Word of God guarantees you'll get your fill of success in life. Good success. Not the kind the world gives, but God's own brand of success.

Success the world's way has a price tag of misery attached to it. But Proverbs 10:22 says, *"The blessing of the Lord, it maketh rich, and he addeth no sorrow with it."*

I will warn you of this, though. Satan won't like it if you choose the way of success. He'll do whatever he can to stop you, and since he knows God's success formula, he knows exactly what tactics to use.

He'll pressure you to say negative things. He'll try to distract you from the Word and get your attention on anything—it doesn't matter what it is, as long as it isn't the Word.

His goal is to stop your faith. He knows it's the only force that can cause impossible situations to change.

He also knows that it comes from the Word of God. So when he sees that Word going in your heart and hears it coming out your mouth, he doesn't just sit there. He starts talking. Doubtful thoughts will come into your mind, thoughts that are just the opposite of what God's Word says.

But those thoughts don't become yours unless you believe them and speak them. That's what he wants you to do, of course. If the Word says you're healed, he'll tell you you're sick. If the Word says you're forgiven, he'll say you're still guilty. If the Word says your needs are met, he'll tell you they're not.

But if you won't let go, if you keep the Word in your mouth and in your heart, you can't lose. There's no force the devil can bring against you that will overcome the Word of God. It will make you a winner every time.

So if you've been wanting good success and it's been eluding you, quit wondering whether you have what it takes to make it— and remember instead Who is with you. Then turn to the Word of God and put God's success formula to work in your life. Start talking it. Start thinking it. Start doing it.

Before long, you won't be chasing success...it will be chasing you!

Change Your Words— Change Your World

"Death and life are in the power of the tongue: and they that love it shall eat the fruit thereof."
— Proverbs 18:21

Edwin Louis Cole

God, Creator of the universe, created people to reflect His image. As the reflection of the Creator, all people have His creative power. When we put God's Word in our mouths and speak His words, those words release creative power into our circumstances that enables us to maintain a high level of Christian living.

It is important that we understand the significance of being made in God's image. One of the differences between us and animals is that though animals can procreate, they have no creative power. Man has a certain measure of God's creative power. Science cannot create, it can only discover what was already created. Researchers discovered the law of gravity and that the world was round. But their discoveries only revealed what originated from God.

Man has the ability to produce beyond the physical senses because of the image in which we were created. Man's creative power is in the image of God's. In other words, just as God released His creative power through words, He has given us the same ability to create through the words we speak. God spoke a word, and the worlds which did not exist suddenly existed (Hebrews 11:3; Romans 4:17). Likewise, man is able to influence the outcome of his life with the words he speaks. Proverbs 18:21 says, *"Death and life are in the power of the tongue: and they that love it shall eat the fruit thereof."*

A man can see a vacant lot and think, *What a great place for an apartment building.* He can think about the apartments and everything it would take to build them and run them, yet still that lot will be vacant. But when he turns to a business partner and says, "We can build apartments there," he begins creating something that did not exist. Once he speaks it, he commits himself to the idea, and together they begin exploring its merits. All the creative force starts with his words.

Use Jesus' Authority

When Jesus Christ walked the earth, He demonstrated the creative power of speaking God's words. The disciples were at sea with Him once when a fierce storm arose. Panic struck. In their terror, the disciples were thrust into a world charged with fear. They were living at the moment in anxiety, tension, stress and impending tragedy. When they woke Jesus—Who was sleeping peacefully—to tell Him of the peril, He stepped onto the bow of the boat and spoke a creative word to the storm: *"Peace, be still"* (Mark 4:39). When Jesus spoke it, the Holy Spirit accomplished it, and there was peace.

Jesus went to a house where a young woman lay dead. He told all the mourners to leave, and He said to the young lady, *"Arise"* (Mark 5:41). At that moment, life arose where there had been lifelessness.

Where there had been the pallor of death, the radiant face of a living soul emerged. His Word created life.

To another person Jesus said, *"Arise, go thy way: thy faith hath made thee whole"* (Luke 17:19). Jesus spoke, and the Spirit brought each of these things into existence.

Jesus had the Spirit of God without measure (John 3:34). We have God's Spirit with measure. When we "die to the flesh" and allow more of the Spirit to indwell us, we have a greater measure of God's Spirit, but none of us experiences God's Spirit without measure as Jesus did. When Jesus spoke, He spoke by the power of the limitless Holy Spirit within Him. He said and did everything God wanted Him to say and do, and it was always by the power of the Holy Spirit. He lived in total dependence upon the Spirit.

But Jesus said a peculiar thing. He said, *"Greater works than these shall he [you] do; because I go unto my Father"* (John 14:12).

Peter understood this delegation of power rather quickly. Days after Jesus had ascended into heaven, Peter went to the temple at the hour of prayer. There he saw a lame man begging, expecting to receive something. Peter said, *"Silver and gold have I none; but such as I have give I thee: In the name of Jesus Christ of Nazareth rise up and walk"* (Acts 3:6).

Using the Name of Jesus, Peter reached out his hand to the beggar and helped him to his feet. And as the Spirit of God confirmed the word which Peter spoke using Jesus' authority, the man leapt to his feet and began walking and jumping. His legs, lame since birth, were suddenly filled with strength and life.

Use Your Word Power to Create Good

Every word we speak is actually a creative word. We create frivolity. We create sobriety. We create strife. We create ease. Our world is constructed by our words, as we saw in Proverbs. Words are potent. They create hurt or health. They create blessing or cursing.

We can speak words of our own and create problems, or speak God's words and create solutions.

We can speak our words and create a hell, or speak God's words and create a heaven.

Jesus said, *"It is the thoughtlife that pollutes. For from within, out of men's hearts, come evil thoughts of lust, theft, murder, adultery, wanting what belongs to others [covetousness], wickedness, deceit, lewdness, envy, slander, pride, and all other folly. All these vile things come from within; they are what pollute [people] and make [them] unfit for God"* (Mark 7:20-23, TLB).

As men speak words of lewdness, deceit, war and animosity, they create the world in which these things exist. The secular world as it exists today was re-created by men whose hearts were apart from the Spirit of God. These men were subject to satanic influence, so when they spoke what was in their hearts, Satan's influence permeated the world. Look at the newspaper. What we see around us is not the world as God created it but the result of man's influence by the words he speaks.

Your words come from your heart.

Whatever is in a person's heart, whatever is in the thought life, will come out in words. No wonder God says He will call every person to account for every *"idle word"* spoken (Matthew 12:36).

When the Spirit of Christ is in us, God gives us His thought life through His Word. Reading God's Word is not a contest for time or length. It is taking in the very life of God through His Word. God gives us the *"mind of Christ"* in and through the Word of God.

As we begin to think God's thoughts, we will begin to speak God's words. As we speak God's words, our world is re-created. It is heavenly! The ingredients of heaven are love, joy, peace, long-suffering, gentleness, goodness, faith, meekness and temperance. These are also known as the *"fruit of the Spirit"* (Galatians 5:22-23). These "fruit" within you come out through your words and are reflected in your world.

The Bible says, "When men say, 'Lo, there is the kingdom of God,' don't go after them. For the kingdom of God isn't here or there. Behold, the kingdom of God is within you" (Luke 17:21, author's paraphrase). By the indwelling of the Spirit of God, the kingdom of God is within you, and the very Word of God becomes your thought life. The Spirit of God becomes the anointing—the life of God in you.

I was in a situation some years ago where I was terribly hurt by others. God took that hurt and changed it into a new thrust of ministry, making something beautiful out of the ashes of my life, according to His Word (Isaiah 61:3). But when I returned a year later to the town where the offense had occurred, I started saying things, making remarks about people who hadn't come to mind since God purged me from the hurt months before. I was losing my peace and joy. Then I realized that I was resurrecting the pain of the situation. I had to control my tongue or else I'd end up speaking words that would revive the entire situation. I knelt down and repented of my words and attitudes. Then I began to confess what God had done for me—how

He had purified me from that failure—and my perception of my life began to change.

I was creating an atmosphere absent from God by saying what I wanted to say according to emotions, feelings, ego, jealousies, hurt and old attitudes. Speaking in obedience to God's thoughts, instead of my own thoughts, changed the situation and restored me to my position of victory.

When God says in His Word that He inhabits the praises of His people (Psalm 22:3), He means that literally. When our hearts overflow with gratitude and thanks to God, we praise Him and fill the air with words and songs, thereby creating an atmosphere in which God's presence is experienced.

Get your heart changed; then let the new words of life flow from you. Negative people will shun you, and positive people will begin to be your friends. They'll bring more positives into your life.

If everyone in the world today repented, received the Spirit of Christ and began to speak only Spirit-inspired words, our world would change. We would have heaven right here on earth. That's what heaven will be like.

Do you have a need, or does someone you know have a problem? Then pray about what to say, and then say it with the authority of Jesus. Let the Holy Spirit bring healing into your life through speaking the words of Jesus. Jesus gave you the authority to speak His words. You are His mouth, His eyes, His hands, His ears. You are the Body of Christ here on earth. Regardless of who is in need, if the Lord gives you a healing word to speak, then speak it in Christ's stead.

Speak words of faith, not fear, and see what God will do!

Live victoriously by being purified from failure, confessing Christ and speaking God's Word. Invest in the study of God's Word and prayer to prepare yourself for your next change or crisis. When you change your heart and change your words, you will change your world.

You may fail from time to time, but if you'll take these principles to heart and never quit, you will become a winner!

God is the author of your success. Trust Him. Be free in Him. Live free.

Winners are not those who never fail, but those who never quit.

The Way of the Winner—Part I

"I press toward the mark for the prize of the high calling of God in Christ Jesus."
— PHILIPPIANS 3:14

Mac Hammond

There's a popular phrase that says, "Winning isn't everything—it's the only thing."

That was definitely my philosophy when I was growing up. From the time I was a small boy, I loved to win and absolutely detested losing. I used to get downright upset over a lost game of marbles!

Later, it was Little League games, swimming and, ultimately, flying in the military. No matter what I was involved in, I wanted to be a winner at it.

I don't think I'm unusual in that respect. I believe most people in our society (at least in secular society) want to be winners.

With believers, it's another story. Somehow, many Christians have been conditioned to believe that winning is not a valid goal for them. They're convinced that winning is unimportant at best and positively unbiblical at worst!

If that's what you've been told, I have news for you. God created you to win, not just spiritually, but in your relationships, your finances, your profession and in every other area of life.

I'll go one step further. If you're not at least in the process of becoming that kind of winner, you're not fulfilling God's whole purpose for your life. And you're missing out on the contentment and sense of fulfillment God wants you to have.

"That's a pretty strong statement, Pastor Mac. Can you back it up with Scripture?" You bet I can.

God Created You to Win

In Genesis 1:26-27 God says: *"Let us make man in our image, after our likeness: and let them have dominion over...all the earth... So God created man in his own image."*

Would you agree that God is a winner? If we are made in His image and likeness, then redeemed man must be designed to be a winner, too.

In fact, after God made Adam and Eve, He commanded them to go win! Look at the very next verse, Genesis 1:28: *"And God blessed them, and God said unto them, Be fruitful, and multiply, and replenish the earth, and subdue it: and have dominion."*

God's very first marching orders to mankind were *"subdue"* and *"have dominion."* In other words, "Go out there and win!"

Likewise, as a born-again, restored child of God, you are to exercise dominion over your world. That means every aspect of daily living—every circumstance in your life—should be in subjection to God.

Winning Ways

OK now. Let's get practical. It's one thing to know that God wants you to be a winner. It's another thing to know how to become one.

Thankfully, God has given us His Word to guide us and great men of faith to be our examples. And when it comes to being a winner, few can teach us more than the Apostle Paul did in his letter to the Philippians.

Philippians is a book about winning, written by a winner. What is it that made Paul such an outstanding winner? I believe we can find the answer to that question in Philippians 3:12-14:

> Not as though I had already attained, either were already perfect: but I follow after, if that I may apprehend that for which also I am apprehended of Christ Jesus. Brethren, I count not myself to have apprehended: but this one thing I do, forgetting those things which are behind, and reaching forth unto those things which are before, I press toward the mark for the prize of the high calling of God in Christ Jesus.

Look again at that last phrase. *"I press toward the mark for the prize of the high calling of God."* A powerful prescription for victory, it contains four terms that represent the keys to finding and fulfilling God's destiny for your life. The terms are *press, mark, prize* and *high calling*. They're the four keys to becoming a winner.

The Press

The winning life isn't a casual stroll. It's a press.

We've heard this term used frequently concerning very spiritual matters. We've been urged to "press in to prayer" or "press in to the Word." And certainly we need to press toward those things. But we mustn't stop there.

Our life is comprised of more than spiritual things alone. Among others, there is a press to make relationships work, a press to keep your body healthy and a press to succeed in business. These are areas that have a very natural, or physical, component to them.

Life itself is a press—a determined movement toward a goal or ideal. Paul knew that. He was a winner because he knew what to press toward—*"the mark for the prize of the high calling of God."*

The Prize

What is the prize of the high calling of God? In a nutshell, it is life—eternal life.

The Greek word the New Testament uses to describe this kind of life is *zoe*. It is a word that refers to the very life of God Himself. And God's Word says you have that life inside of you if you're a born-again believer.

Too often, we think of eternal life as beginning in heaven. But that's simply not the case. Our eternal life has already begun. It is here and now.

Furthermore, *zoe* refers to a quality of life as well as a "forever" length of life. It literally means, "life as God has it."

Does God experience sickness, poverty, strife-filled relationships, unforgiveness or bitterness? Of course not.

I realize it may seem almost sacrilegious to your natural mind, yet that kind of life—the life of God Himself—is the prize

Paul is talking about. That's the prize God has made available to us, not just in heaven but right here on earth. It can be ours now!

The High Calling of God

To really experience the fullness of *zoe* life this side of heaven, you'll have to lay hold of God's high calling. What is that high calling? It's different for each of us.

Basically, your high calling is God's perfect will for your life. It is your divine destiny. It's being in the place for which He uniquely created you.

Please understand, I'm talking about much more here than just finding the right career. God's high calling touches every area of your existence. Certainly it involves your vocation, but also it includes your relationships, your health and your material wealth.

God's high calling is a wonderful place to be. It is a place of all-sufficiency. It is a place of great influence. It is a place of supernatural health and harmonious relationships.

Most of all, reaching God's high calling means realizing and living the dream that He has placed in your heart.

That dream may be crystal clear to you. Or it may be only a vague idea stirring in your heart. It may even be that you don't yet have the foggiest notion of what God created you to do.

But don't worry! As long as you are moving in the right direction, you'll eventually find your high calling. So just look for "the mark" and go.

The Mark

In many respects, the concept of "the mark" is the most important of all in Paul's statement about "pressing toward the mark of the high calling."

Notice that Paul didn't say, "I press toward the prize." Nor did he say he was pressing toward the high calling. No, it is the mark that he has his sights set on, but why?

The mark, as Paul describes it here, is an intermediate goal or objective. If you'll focus on it and move toward it, it will keep you on course.

If you know anything about bowling, you know that each lane has on it a series of marks that lie just a few feet in front of the bowler. Good bowlers use these marks to aim the ball so that it ultimately strikes the pins in the proper place. The bowler doesn't aim at the pins—he focuses on the mark.

That's what Paul is talking about here. You may not yet know what your high calling is. The dream God has placed in your heart may not be defined well enough for you to know what to do next. But, praise God, His Word has given us a mark to press toward. Head for that mark and ultimately God's dream or "high calling" for you will come into view.

The Mark: Service

There is one interesting thing about this "mark." It is the same for all of us no matter how widely our individual callings may vary. It is a universal signpost that will put all who follow it on the pathway of the winner.

What is this mark that we must press toward? In a word, it is servanthood.

Jesus, the ultimate Winner, established that with His words and with His example. Remember when the disciples were arguing about who among them was the greatest? Jesus told them that the greatest among them was he who would be the servant of all. Later He demonstrated that principle by washing their feet.

Service is the key to becoming a winner. It's the mark by which we should measure every decision, every action and every thought.

The problem is, many of us have a negative, stereotypical image of what a servant is. We equate servanthood with slavery and forced servitude. We think the role of the servant is degrading and certainly not something we equate with winning.

But if you're going to win the prize of true *zoe* life, you're going to have to change the way you think about servanthood. You're going to have to realize that it is the way of the winner.

When you begin serving with your money (in other words, giving), you'll soon find yourself winning in the area of finances. Start serving in the area of relationships (loving), and you'll soon reap a winning harvest of love in your own life.

The same principle applies to any and every area of your existence. The more you press toward the mark of service, the more you'll find yourself moving into God's marvelous *zoe* life. Your every step will bring you closer to the center of God's will because, at last, you'll be walking the way of the winner!

A Matter of Choice

*"Let the wicked forsake his
way, and the unrighteous man
his thoughts."*
— ISAIAH 55:7

Kenneth
Copeland

"It doesn't matter how hard I try, everything I do turns out wrong!"

Have you ever felt that way? I certainly have. There was a time in my life when everything I put my hand to fell apart. Back then, I chalked it up to "bad luck."

But I was wrong.

I've found out in the more than 30 years since then, there's no such thing as luck—good or bad. In fact, I've taken the term completely out of my vocabulary.

It's not luck that determines how things turn out in our lives—it's choices. When we make really good ones, things go well for us. When we make bad ones, things go wrong.

No doubt, some folks would dispute that. They'd tell me about times when they did everything right. Times when they gathered all the information, listened to the experts and made a wise choice that, due to circumstances beyond their control, got them in trouble.

But the truth is, no matter how "right" you think you were at the time, a decision that brings trouble is a poor decision.

"Oh, but Brother Copeland, there's no way in the world I could have known in advance what would happen in that situation!"

No, there may not have been any way in this natural world you could have made a better choice. But, if you're a born-again believer, you aren't restricted to making choices according to this natural world. You have another, far more powerful option.

Don't Just Bail—Believe!

Look at Mark 4 and you'll see what I mean. There, we find Jesus' disciples facing a problem that required them to take some kind of action. But they chose the wrong action—and it landed them in deep water.

Here's the situation. Jesus had been preaching all day at the seaside. At the end of the day, He had instructed the disciples to take Him by boat to the other side of the sea.

> And when they [the disciples] had sent away the multitude, they took him [Jesus] even as he was in the ship...And there arose a great storm of wind, and the waves beat into the ship, so that it was now full. And he was in the hinder part of the ship, asleep on a pillow: and they awake him, and say unto him, Master, carest thou not that we perish? And he arose, and rebuked the wind, and said unto the sea, Peace, be still. And the wind ceased, and there was a great calm. And he said unto them, Why are ye so fearful? how is it that ye have no faith? And they feared exceedingly, and said one to another, What manner of man is this, that even the wind and the sea obey him? (Mark 4:36-41).

Now, think about this situation for a moment. There were the disciples, facing this fierce storm. No doubt they were doing everything they knew to do, naturally speaking, to keep their boat afloat. They were bailing, they were paddling.

But they didn't say a word to Jesus, even though He was right there in the boat with them!

They didn't call on His power until the boat was full of water and they were about to sink. Why? They'd made the wrong choice. They had chosen to look to natural solutions instead of supernatural ones. Faith never even entered their minds until they were about to drown!

It should have. After all, Jesus had been teaching them the Word all day. He'd told them how the devil comes to choke the Word with pressures and cares of the world. Then he got into the boat and said, "Now we will go to the other side," and went to sleep expecting His Word to be carried out.

If they'd really listened to the Word Jesus had taught, any one of those disciples could have—and should have—stood up in the bow of that boat and hollered, "Peace, be still! The Son of the living God has told us to go to the other side of this lake, and we are going if we have to walk!"

If they'd thought supernaturally, instead of just naturally, any one of them could have drawn by faith on the Anointing and the words of Jesus and stopped that storm. But they made the wrong choice.

Many well-meaning believers are making that same mistake today. They have Jesus right there in their boat, but they're depending on natural resources to get them through their lives instead of calling on the supernatural Anointing of God. They're making the wrong choices, so they're going under.

A Supernatural Mind

Actually, it never occurred to the disciples to take the supernatural way out of that situation. It never entered their minds to stand up and speak to that storm. The reason is simple. They didn't think as Jesus thought.

51

He thought like Someone Who had access at all times to the power of God Himself, which is superior to all the forces of the natural world. (That's why it's called supernatural.) The disciples thought like people who were subject to those natural forces.

That's why they *"feared exceedingly, and said one to another, What manner of man is this, that even the wind and the sea obey him?"*

Instead of jumping up and saying, "Hey, that's the way I want to be!" they just thought Jesus was strange. People still think that about God. They say things like, "You never know what God will do. He moves in mysterious ways."

That was true until the Holy Spirit came to teach us all things. (See John 16:13.) We're not meant to look at God as some strange, mysterious being anymore. We're to know Him and imitate Him as dearly beloved children (Ephesians 5:1).

The truth is, He isn't strange at all. He has just seemed strange to us because instead of living on His level as we were created to do, mankind has slipped down into the natural realm in his thinking. When you're living at that low level, everything about God baffles you.

Some folks say, "Yes, amen, but you know that's the way the Bible says it will be. After all, God's ways are higher than our ways and His thoughts than our thoughts."

Yes, it does, and if that's all it said, we could never hope to be anything except stupid. But, praise God, the Bible doesn't stop there. If you'll go ahead and read the rest of Isaiah 55, you'll find God also said:

> **As the rain cometh down, and the snow from heaven, and returneth not thither, but watereth the earth, and maketh it bring forth and bud, that it may give seed to the sower, and bread to the eater: So shall my word be that goeth forth out of my mouth: it shall not return unto me void, but it shall accomplish that which I please, and it shall prosper in the thing whereto I sent it (verses 10-11).**

In other words, you don't have to stay below God's thoughts. Your thoughts can come up to His level. How? Through His Word. God's thoughts are in His Word, so if you think His Word, you'll think His thoughts.

But wait a minute. To think God's supernatural thoughts, you'd have to have a "supernatural mind" wouldn't you?

Yes—and if you're a believer, you already have one. First Corinthians 2:16 says it this way: *"We have the mind of Christ."* I read that for years, but I didn't really understand it until I translated the word *Christ.* It means "the Anointed One."

So, to have the mind of Christ is to have a mind that is under the influence of the Anointing of God.

A mind that's not under the influence of God is in opposition to Him. It always goes contrary to His ways. And since God's ways are right, then a mind without the anointing will think wrong.

Twisted or Transformed?

That's why Isaiah 55:7 says, *"Let the wicked forsake his way, and the unrighteous man his thoughts."* The word *wicked* there actually means "twisted."

Satan takes God's thoughts and twists them. He takes the truth and turns it into a lie. Thus, people who don't have the Anointing of God on their minds have twisted thinking. They are thinking Satan's thoughts.

They don't realize that, of course. They think they're thinking their own thoughts. But in reality, they don't have that option.

You see, as members of the race of man, you and I are not independent entities. We are spirit and we are created in God's class, or image, but we are not sovereign. We are not God.

Each one of us has a spiritual Lord. If we choose Jesus, He is our Lord. Those who don't choose Jesus have the devil as their lord by default, whether they acknowledge it or not.

Since we are not independent entities, we cannot have independent thoughts. We will either be thinking Satan's thoughts or God's thoughts. The straight thoughts of God are truth and the twisted thoughts of the devil are lies, and there is nothing in between.

But, let me warn you. Just because you've made Jesus your Lord doesn't mean you'll automatically think God's thoughts. You only begin thinking God's thoughts when you begin to fill your mind and heart with the Word of God and make yourself subject to His Anointing.

Romans 12:2 calls that process *"the renewing of your mind."* It also says that process will transform you. Why does it have such a dramatic effect? Because when you change your mind, you change your choices—and that changes everything!

Immersed in the Word

I'll never forget when that transformation began in me. I had just begun to learn what the Word of God and faith can do. I was so hungry for it and so desperate to change my life that I completely immersed myself in it.

I kept teaching and preaching tapes going all the time. I'd get up in the morning and put on a tape while I was shaving. I'd carry the recorder to the table and listen while I ate breakfast. Then I'd haul it out to the car (that was back in the days of the big reel-to-reel recorders, so "haul" is a fairly accurate term) and listen to it while I drove to school. When I got back home at night, I listened to the Word again until I fell asleep.

I was 30 years old at that time and I'd pretty much thought the same way all my life—a way that had maneuvered me into more messes than I could find any natural way out of.

But after just a few days of constantly feeding on the Word, I began to notice a change. My mind started working differently. I found myself comparing everything I heard, whether it came out of my mouth or someone else's, with the Word of God.

When I'd hear something that was out of line with the Word, it would be glaringly apparent to me. Somebody would ask me how I was feeling. Instead of saying those old things I used to say—"Well, you know this old football injury has really been acting up lately. It's giving me this shooting pain right up my leg"—I would just explode with the Word of God.

I'd say, "What difference does it make how I feel? I am not moved by what I feel. I am not moved by what I see. I am moved by what I believe and I believe the Word of God!" I just jumped on people like a chicken on a bug. (I didn't know any better back then. Thank God, He's mellowed me some over the years.)

What was happening? The anointing, the influence of God and His Word, was on my mind. It was teaching me things.

The Bible says if you'll meditate on the Word day and night, it will talk to you when you wake up in the morning and visit with you all day long. That's exactly what it began to do with me all those years ago.

I'd make choices with ease that other people struggled over. The Word made it clear for me which route I should take. I didn't have to agonize or debate over what I should do; the Word working in me caused me to make the right choice.

A Supernatural Choice

One of the best examples I've ever seen of the Word determining someone's choice was in my dad's life. When I was just a teenager, he was called to testify in a lawsuit his company had brought against a man who had broken contract with them to begin his own company.

There was a great deal of money on the line and the man had already offered my dad millions of dollars' worth of stock in his company if he would testify in his favor. All my dad had to give was a yes or no answer. If he said no, he walked out of the courtroom a multimillionaire. If he said yes, he walked out with his job intact and a pat on the back.

He didn't even have to think about it. He just walked in the courtroom, answered yes and ended the lawsuit.

Afterward, I asked Dad, "How could you say that and just walk away from all that money?"

He answered simply, "Because to say anything else would have been a lie."

My dad didn't experience any pressure in that situation. As far as he was concerned, there was only one thing to do. His choice had been made by the Word of God long before he ever stepped into the courtroom. He'd already made a decision that lying was not in his lifestyle and his choice flowed out of that decision.

Somebody might say, "Boy, that would be a tough choice to make." No, it would be harder than tough—it would be supernatural.

You have to be living above this natural realm to turn down an "easy" multimillion dollars. But you can do it if the Word of God is abiding in you.

Notice I said "abiding." That's the term Jesus used when referring to His Word. He said, *"If ye abide in me, and my words abide in you, ye shall ask what ye will, and it shall be done unto you"* (John 15:7). The word *abide* means "to live."

God's words are living forces. Powerful forces that, if you allow them to take up residence in you, will produce holiness in your life.

To be holy is to be separated to God's use. Therefore, if you'll allow your choices to be bathed in the anointing of God's Word, those choices will separate you from the destructive bent of this natural world and take you into the blessings of the SUPERnatural realm.

Just think how far-reaching the consequences of such a change would be. Your choices can affect an entire generation. You can make certain choices that can either damage or enrich lives all around you. What may not seem like a very important decision to you may ultimately make vital differences in your own future and that of your family.

But God sees the whole picture. He knows what's around the corner that you can't see. So when you are walking in His choices, your life starts to fit. Things start working. All the pieces of the puzzle start coming together.

You can save yourself so much heart-ache and headache it isn't even funny, just by spending some quality time in God's presence and in His Word. If you'll let Him, He will help you with every choice you make.

No Natural Solutions

Yes, every choice. Such a thought would surprise most people. They have an idea that they'll bring God in on the major problems in their lives but handle the other things fine without Him.

It's kind of a personal version of the government's "separation of church and state" theory. If you want to know how well that theory works, take a look at how the government is doing. It can't pay its bills, can't control crime, can't keep its citizens healthy... you know the story.

The fact is, natural power can't keep things from going downhill. No matter how many natural choices you try, nothing works.

Here's the reason. What we call the natural world is really "subnatural." It is far below what God originally created it to be.

When God created the earth, things were perfect. There was a water canopy that covered it and filtered out ultraviolet light, among other things. The atmospheric pressure was greater; the oxygen level was higher. People lived an average of 12 times longer (see Genesis 2:6, 5, 7:10-11; 2 Peter 3:5-6).

But the effect of sin on the earth eventually caused that canopy to explode and flood the earth. Noah and his family were the only ones who survived.

The loss of that canopy dramatically damaged Earth's atmosphere. Add to that damage the sin and destruction Satan has wrought and you'll realize why you have a basic, fundamental need to choose the supernatural rather than the natural.

It's necessary to your well-being in every area of life!

You were born into an atmosphere you weren't created to live in. You face situations you weren't created to handle. You constantly encounter problems to which there are no natural solutions.

To have abundant life on this death-bound planet, you'll have to live a SUPER-natural lifestyle by making SUPERnatural choices every day of your life!

If you'll do that, it won't matter that this world is constantly bringing forth new kinds of danger and destruction—you can live on the Word of God in health, strength and victory for 120 years if you want (Genesis 6:3).

Instead of talking about getting old, you can talk the 103rd Psalm. Every morning when you get in the shower, you can get the washcloth in one hand, the soap in the other and start talking the Word. Stand under the water and say, "Praise God, He fills my mouth with good things so my youth is renewed like the eagle's!"

Every time you do something like that, you're making a supernatural choice. A choice to live by the Word rather than to die like the world.

Start now getting that Word into your heart. Start now letting the force of it and the anointing upon it direct your choices— big and small. Let God begin to lift you up to His way of thinking.

Then when the storms of life come, you'll know what to do. Instead of just grabbing a bucket and starting to bail, faith will rise up within you and you'll say, "Look here, storm. Peace, be still."

It will work for you just as it would have worked for the disciples. After all, you have Jesus in your boat!

The Secret to Getting Ahead

"Wisdom is the principal thing; therefore get wisdom: and with all thy getting get understanding. Exalt her, and she shall promote thee: she shall bring thee to honour, when thou dost embrace her."

— PROVERBS 4:7-8

Gloria Copeland

From this moment on, I want you to stop thinking of the Bible as a storybook. I want you to stop thinking of it as a religious textbook. I want you to stop thinking of it as a history book. I want you to start thinking of it as a handbook for living.

That's what it is, you know. It's the wisdom of Almighty God written down for you so you can apply it to your life and circumstances.

Consistently read and applied, the Bible will turn you into a winner. Not just now and then. Not just here and there. But every day in every single area of your life!

Does that sound too good to be true?

Then don't take my word for it. Let the Lord speak for Himself. In Proverbs 4:7-8, He says, *"For skillful and godly Wisdom is the principal thing...Prize Wisdom highly and exalt her, and she will exalt and promote you; she will bring you to honor when you embrace her"* (AMP).

Be advised, though, this promise isn't meant for those who want to dab a little of the Word on their lives now and then when they get in a scrape. It's talking about those who are willing to put the Word of God first place in their lives day after day after day!

Look again at the first part of that scripture. *"Skillful and godly Wisdom is the principal thing." Principal* means "first in importance." According to that verse, you're going to have to make God's Word the most important thing in your life. Instead of being content with an occasional scanning of the Bible, you're going to have to develop a passion for it. You'll have to prize the Word highly, putting it before all your other activities.

When you do that, God promises that the Word will exalt and promote you and bring you to honor. Who could ask for anything more?

There are two very practical ways to give the Word first place in your life.

First, plan your daily schedule around the Word instead of trying to squeeze the Word into your daily schedule. As you mentally plan each day, automatically set aside time to study the Word first.

I know from experience what an impact that can have on your life. More than 20 years ago, I heard a great man of God—Oral Roberts—say that the Lord had instructed him to read the Gospels and the book of Acts three times in 30 days in order to get a greater revelation of Jesus. That inspired me to do the same thing.

I knew the Lord wanted me to begin at once—but it could not have been a more inopportune time.

We had just moved to Tulsa so that Kenneth could attend Oral Roberts University. Everything at our house was still upside down. We hadn't even finished unpacking.

In addition to all that, I had the children to care for. Both were at demanding ages. Kellie was 3 years old and John was 9 months. When they wanted something, they wouldn't wait 30 minutes, much less 30 days!

Where will I get the time? I wondered.

Still, I was determined. No matter what it took, I was going to read the Gospels and Acts three times in 30 days.

I figured how many pages I needed to read a day in my Amplified Bible. It came to four hours or more daily. Most of the reading had to be done while the children were asleep, so I set time aside three times a day. Rising at 5:30 a.m., I read until the rest of the family woke up. When the children took their naps in the afternoon, I read again. Then at night, I would finish whatever was left.

Regardless of what happened or what needed to be done, I put God's Word first. I thought the other things would just have to wait until next month, but God had a pleasant surprise in store for me!

On the very first day, I sat down at 3 o'clock in the afternoon with my day's work done—and I had already spent several hours in the Word! On the following days, I continued to put God's Word first. And by the end of the month, I'd painted and antiqued four pieces of furniture from start to finish, done the ironing (which had been accumulating for weeks) and gotten my house in order.

I was amazed. I would never have been able to do that under normal conditions!

Back then, Kenneth and I knew very little about how to live by faith. I didn't know that the Word makes your way prosperous and causes good success (Joshua 1:8, AMP). I didn't know that if you put God's wisdom first, it would exalt and promote you.

But I experienced a miracle of God just the same. By faith, I had put His Word first, and He caused Proverbs 4:7-8 to come to pass in my life.

He'll do the same for you! Whether you're a housewife, a mechanic or an executive, once you commit yourself to making God's

Word your first priority, you'll begin to prosper in everything you do.

But let me warn you, you'll never get around to the Word if you wait until you have time. Satan will see to it that you never have the time. He is vehemently opposed to your feeding on God's Word.

So learn to set aside less important things. Start giving the Word first place in your schedule and everything else will fall in line. Jesus knew that. That's why He said, *"Seek ye first the kingdom of God, and his righteousness; and all these things shall be added unto you"* (Matthew 6:33).

Guard your time in the Word. Satan will steal it from you if he can. He'll use everything from television to church activities to lure you away from God's wisdom.

Why? Because he knows that the Word makes you free from his dominion! If he can keep you out of the Word, he can keep you bound and struggling.

Putting the Word first is something you'll have to do continually. When you get bogged down in the details of living, when you find yourself frustrated by failures big and small, check the amount of time you're spending in the Word. You'll find that you've let the Word slip into second place and spent your Word time on other things.

That's what happened to Martha. Jesus Himself was in her living room teaching the Word. But she didn't think she had time to listen. She was too busy cooking dinner for Him. I'm sure it seemed like the only proper thing for her to do. After all, Jesus and His ministry team were staying in her home. Let's read that passage.

> Now it came to pass, as they went, that he entered into a certain village: and a certain woman named Martha received him into her house. And she had a sister called Mary, which also sat at Jesus' feet, and heard his word. But Martha was cumbered about much serving, and came to him, and said, Lord, dost thou not care that my sister hath left me to serve alone? bid her therefore that she help me. And Jesus answered and said unto

her, Martha, Martha, thou art careful and troubled about many things: But one thing is needful: and Mary hath chosen that good part, which shall not be taken away from her (Luke 10:38-42).

I can just see Martha stewing around the kitchen, banging pots and pans feeling sorry for herself. She wanted Jesus to rebuke Mary, but instead the Master was pleased that Mary had put His Word first.

Martha could have been at the Master's feet too, if she'd made up her mind to be. Jesus had fed thousands with a few loaves and fish. He could have just as easily prepared a banquet for all those present that day!

You may think, *What an opportunity Martha wasted! I would never do that.* But every time you allow things to swallow up your time in the Word, you're passing up the opportunity to sit at the Master's feet, just as she did.

In addition to building your schedule around the Word of God, there's a second way to give the Word priority in your life: by acting on it!

Simply acquiring knowledge of the Word isn't enough. You're going to have to put that knowledge to work in your life before it's going to bring results. I can sit around knowing how to turn on a light all night long, but until I apply that knowledge by getting up and flipping the switch, I'll be in the dark.

The Word of God works the same way. So as soon as you learn something from it, take action. Do it!

Then, as you see the wisdom of the Word produce results in your life, you'll begin to esteem and prize wisdom above all that you may desire in life (Proverbs 3:15). And as you put the Word first and exalt it in your life, the Word will exalt and promote you.

Start today. Spend some quality time in God's Word. Make that the first and most important item on your agenda. Your daily activities will go more smoothly. And as you continually apply the wisdom you glean from God's Word, you'll find yourself moving ahead daily in every area of life. *"This book of the law shall not depart out of your mouth, but you shall meditate on it day and night, that you may observe and do according to all that is written in it; for then you shall make your way prosperous, and then you shall deal wisely and have good success"* (Joshua 1:8, AMP). Good success belongs to you.

Your Vision Is the Blueprint

Chapter 6

"If thou canst believe, all things are possible to him that believeth."
— Mark 9:23

George Pearsons

Are you making plans for the holidays or a vacation? Perhaps you'll be traveling somewhere—to your hometown to visit a friend or to the mountains or the beach. Maybe you will spend quiet time at home, or friends or family will be coming to your house.

Whatever your plans are, start to see that event before you now. Are you getting excited about it? Do you have the vision of it happening? Can you picture it in your heart?

When my family and I make plans for vacations or holidays, there are numerous arrangements to make, such as ordering airline tickets or making hotel reservations. Sometimes the preparations seem endless.

But as the fulfillment of that vision draws closer, a new excitement builds within me.

I can see the winter snow coming down back home on Cape Cod at Christmas. I look forward to being with my parents or seeing my sister again. I have a vision for spending time with my children or sharing special time with my wife, Terri.

As I've thought about this, it has occurred to me that if we can catch a vision for the events in our lives, how much more should we have a vision for heaven and the things of God?

How much more should we long to see our churches filled so that we are continually building larger auditoriums with bigger altars and more seating.

We should be a people of vision.

Faith and Vision: The Connection

Proverbs 29:18 says, *"Where there is no vision, the people perish: but he that keepeth the law, happy is he."* Other translations say, *"Where there is no vision, the people go wild,"* or *"go out of their minds."*

Also, when you read the word "law," the word "commandment" or the word "precept" in Scripture, it is referring to the Word of God. So without changing its meaning, turn this verse around and it can very easily be translated to read, "Where there is vision, the people prosper, and he that keeps the Word of God will walk in joy."

The one thing God has given us to help maintain an enthusiasm of faith is to be able to look toward the future and see the vision.

And everyone must have a vision. The vision you need is found in the Word of God because the Word lays out our potential for us: What God's Word says we can do, we can do. What it says we can have, we can have. What it says we can be, we can be.

Our potential is built in the Word of God. And that's where you begin with your vision. If you don't yet have a vision, you start where God has told you who you are in Him.

It's Your Choice

I thank God that it doesn't matter who we are in ourselves. It only matters who we are in Him. That's the difference between being self-conscious and being God-conscious.

God always gives you a choice.

You can choose to be aware of God and what He wants you to do, or you can choose to be aware of yourself and do your own thing. Personally, I'd rather be doing God's thing.

But to do God's thing, you must realize that your vision is found in the Word of God. And the details of that vision come by setting aside time every day to be in His presence—in intimate fellowship with the Father. The vision is conceived in those times. The vision is nurtured in those times. And also, the vision is birthed in those times.

When you never take time for intimate fellowship with the Father, you'll never get the details. It's hard to get details on the run. You have to have a face-to-face relationship to do that.

And guess what? He wants you to have vision. He wants to give you details.

Not only that, but He also wants to enlarge the vision so that you are filled with it. God likes big vision.

Eagle Mountain International Church, where I pastor, recently completed the construction of our new, 1500-seat auditorium. And to be honest with you, I saw that building completely built even before one wall went up. I had that vision. The closer it came to being finished, the more excited I became, the more details I received from the Father and the easier it was to see the vision completed.

But the vision didn't stop when we dedicated the building and everyone showed up for the first Sunday service. No way! I see the completion of this building as a step toward a much larger building.

Sometimes you can be encouraged by watching people who you know are fulfilling the vision God has given them. Before John Osteen went to be with the Lord, I used to get so encouraged when I watched his television program. The way the church building was set up, and the way that camera followed him on the platform while he was preaching, you could see all of the people in the church. And I loved to look at the people.

In Mark 9:23, Jesus said, *"If thou canst believe, all things are possible to him that believeth."* All things are possible to anyone who believes.

You have to be willing to not listen to anyone who wants to speak doubt and unbelief to you. You have to take the word "doubt" out of your vocabulary. Instead, align your vocabulary with heaven's vocabulary...align your vocabulary to faith's vocabulary...align your vocabulary to the Word of God.

Your vision—the vision that God has given you, the vision that God is building in your heart—is possible. Why? Because you believe.

Even when you can't see it, you believe it. Even when you can't touch it, you believe it. And the highest kind of faith is faith that believes on the authority of the Word of God alone, and does not demand evidence to know that it's true. That's the centurion kind of faith.

Great Faith

Remember the centurion who came to Jesus and said, *"my servant lieth at home sick"*? When Jesus answered him saying, *"I will come and heal him,"* the centurion said, *"Lord, I am not worthy that thou shouldest come under my roof: but speak the word only, and my servant shall be healed"* (Matthew 8:6-8).

The Word of God says when Jesus heard that statement, He marveled at this man's faith. This man was operating in the highest realm of faith—the faith that does not demand evidence. Jesus called it *"so great faith"* (verse 10).

Sometimes I say to myself, "I believe. I'm a believer. I believe the Word of God. I believe it in the Name of Jesus."

You have to say those words to yourself every now and then. You have to say them over and over again because sometimes the circumstances around you just don't look like they agree with the vision.

Remember, the vision in your heart is possible to those who believe. Your faith is inseparable from your vision. Whatever vision you have on the inside—whether it's a small, medium or large vision—your faith is going to work to produce that vision.

The spiritual force of the faith which is on the inside of you will take those pictures and those images from deep within your heart and begin to produce the vision and bring it to pass. Your vision is the blueprint of whatever your faith wants to build. And the builder works from that blueprint. *"Faith is the substance* [the ground, the title deed] *of things hoped for,* [the things I have a red-hot, burning, earnest expectation and a vision for]" (Hebrews 11:1).

That scripture says my faith is the evidence of my vision, and your faith is the evidence of your vision. It's the evidence of things that you have a red-hot, burning, earnest expectation for.

Your faith wants to build your vision. Your faith is just as determined as the kid on the football team who is sitting on the bench saying, "Coach, let me in. Let me play. Let me get in there."

Keep It Before Your Eyes

Do you have a vision? Can you see it? What are you doing to supplement and supply the vision that you have on the inside of you? Because whatever it is, that's what you will eventually achieve. That's what you will become.

Terri and I have been believing God for a new home. We need a larger house, so we thank God for the house that we have and thank Him that we have a roof over our heads. But, yet, we have a vision for a bigger home.

Well, there's a magazine that we receive on a regular basis—it's one of those unique type of homes magazines. And as I started looking through it one day, I noticed a house that cost $1.8 million. Another house cost $1.9 million, and a third was $3.2 million. They were pretty nice homes, too.

I used to look through that magazine and be intimidated by prices like these. I'd think, *This is just too far beyond me.*

But, you see, there's a place where you use your faith, and there's a place where you step where it is too far beyond you right at this moment. Just as you learn to walk by taking one step at a time, you also have to take steps in your faith. And there is nothing wrong with enlarging your vision. God wants you to think big.

I was looking at some beautiful houses in that magazine one day and noticed that in one of them, there was a study that I really liked. So I cut out the picture. Now, I'm building a house on my refrigerator with cutouts from the magazine.

Take a Clue

You have to keep the vision alive and before you.

We could take a clue from how the world uses this principle in their marketing and advertising. They use the print media (billboards, the sides of buses and signs in airports) and television—what the public sees. They use radio—what the public hears. We are surrounded with people who are trying to convince us to think the way they think and telling us to go buy what they are selling.

This is the idea: If you see it enough, you'll buy it. And then you'll like it.

This same principle works in the Word of God. If you're putting the world in front of you, you are going to become like the world. If you put the Word in front of you, you'll become like the Word. We must be extremely selective in what we put in front of our eyes.

The enemy tries to deceive us by building images and visions before us, even from the time we are children. He'll show us visions and pictures of our parents or our grandparents who are in lack or are poor and doing without. Since that image is constantly before us, we think we should live that way. The devil puts an image of failure, defeat, worry and fear before us. But the Word of God gives us an image of success, victory, abundance and peace.

What are you going to keep before you? What you behold, what you look at, what you meditate on and what you think about are what you are going to become.

Second Corinthians 3:12-13 says, *"Since we have such [glorious] hope—such [joyful and confident] expectation—we speak very freely and openly and fearlessly. Nor [do we act] like Moses, who put a veil over his face so that the Israelites might not gaze upon the finish of the vanishing [splendor which had been upon it]"* (AMP).

In other words, Moses would go up into the mountain to talk with the Lord. Then he would put a veil over his face, come down the mountain and then talk to the people. But he would keep the veil over his face, and the glory began to wane and diminish:

> In fact, their minds were grown hard and calloused—they had become dull and had lost the power of understanding; for until this present day, when the Old Testament [the old covenant] is being read, that same veil still lies [on their hearts], not being lifted [to reveal] that in Christ it is made void and done away. Yes, down to this [very]

day whenever Moses is read a veil lies upon their minds and hearts.

But whenever a person turns (in repentance) to the Lord the veil is stripped off and taken away. Now the Lord is the Spirit, and where the Spirit of the Lord is, there is liberty—emancipation from bondage, freedom. And all of us, as with unveiled face, [because we] continued to behold [look, see, focus our eyes upon and continue to look at] [in the Word of God] as in a mirror the glory of the Lord, are constantly being transfigured (verses 14-18, AMP).

If there are some things that you know you should not be exposing yourself to, cut them out of your life—for the sake of the anointing, for the sake of the glory of God, for the sake of the vision. Get rid of them.

The force of faith is working within you to conform you to whatever image you are seeing. It is working to bring your vision to pass. And as you behold the Word of God, and you behold the glory of the

Word, you will, in increasing splendor, go from glory to glory.

You will become what you behold.

Taking Your Cues

"Awake, O sleeper, and arise from the dead...Live purposefully and worthily and accurately, not as the unwise and witless, but as wise— sensible, intelligent people."
— EPHESIANS 5:14-15, AMP

Lynne Hammond

Emergency hours are coming upon the world. Hours that will require God's people to be a praying people. When I say "praying people," I'm not talking about people who just pray aimless, namby-pamby kinds of prayers. I'm talking about people who know how to pray supernaturally and bring the power of God to bear in a situation.

Where prayer is concerned, you and I can't afford to be "airheads." The Bible says it this way: *"Awake, O sleeper, and arise from the dead...Live purposefully and worthily and accurately, not as the unwise and witless, but as wise—sensible, intelligent people"* (Ephesians 5:14-15, AMP). In other words, don't be an airhead. Instead, pray purposefully and accurately.

How? I could preach for months in answer to that question. But for now, I just want to look briefly with you at three elements that are essential to supernatural prayer: faith, the Word and the Holy Spirit.

Faith

Hebrews 11:6 says, *"Without faith it is impossible to please [God]."* In recent times, some people in the Body of Christ have tried to separate the prayer of faith from other kinds of prayers and put it in a category by itself. But the truth is, you always, always have to travel in faith no matter what kind of praying you are doing.

I like to think of faith as the vehicle that gets your prayers where they're going. If you don't use that vehicle, they won't ever get there. What's more, the higher your faith level is, the faster and more effective your prayers will be. You might say the level of your faith will determine whether they go by pony express or by the space shuttle.

So to pray supernaturally, you're going to have to constantly cultivate your faith by staying in the Word of God.

The Word

There is no way to overemphasize the importance of the Word of God in your prayer life. In John 15:7 Jesus said, *"If ye abide in me, and my words abide in you, ye shall ask what ye will, and it shall be done unto you."*

What does it mean to live in Him and have His words remain in you? It means you're so full of His Word that when you come up against a problem in prayer, you latch onto the word God has given you about that problem and remain steadfast in that Word. You meditate on it and refuse to let go of it.

You see, when God gives you an assignment to pray for a specific situation, He'll always give you scriptures that show you how that situation is going to be resolved. He won't give you scriptures that reflect the problem the person is going through. He'll give you the scriptures that reflect the victory that's coming. He'll give you a promise to hold onto.

Those are the words that remain in you—and those are the words you pray. You don't pray the problems. That's the earthly part. You pray the heavenly part. You pray the victory.

I once heard someone say that when a black belt in karate stands in front of a stack of boards and prepares to split them wide open, he doesn't focus his attention on the boards. If he were to do that, he wouldn't break through them. He puts his focus down through the floor. That way the energy of his blow will take him right on through the boards to his point of focus.

It's the same way with prayer. You settle in on the Word of God deeper and deeper until it becomes implanted so deeply that you can't see that situation any other way. That is what the Bible calls "fervent" prayer, and it says it's a very powerful thing (James 5:16).

There is a story about George Mueller, a great man of God in the last century, which illustrates that kind of prayer very well. Mr. Mueller prayed for 57 years for a certain man's salvation—without any apparent success. Yet when someone asked him if he had any doubts as to whether the man would ever be saved, Mueller said he had none at all. He said he was as certain of that man's salvation as if he'd seen him standing before the throne of God. Sure enough, the man was saved at George Mueller's funeral.

Flowing With the Holy Spirit

You need to understand one thing: Time is not a factor for God. We live in such a fast-paced world that everyone seems to want what they want instantly. They want God to do this or that right now. That doesn't work with God.

When I pray, I spend as much time just abiding in God as I do praying. Sometimes I only pray 15 or 20 minutes, but I've spent a lot of time just fellowshiping with the Lord and letting Him put things into my spirit.

This is where we miss it so much of the time. We get up in the morning and say, "O, God, guide me today in my daily affairs." But when it comes to prayer, we don't want to have to wait on God and get direction from Him. That takes too long. We just want to jump out there and do whatever seems best to us.

Not only is it vital to give God time, but you need to learn to cooperate with the Holy Spirit when you pray. Prayer doesn't come from your head. It comes from your heart by the power of the Holy Ghost.

But before you can pray from your heart, you have to find out what's in there. You have to locate what is in your own heart. You can't pray from what is in someone else's heart.

A few years ago, we had some seasoned prayer warriors in our church. A few other people started looking at what they did and said, "That's spiritual, so I'm going to do what they do."

Here is the mistake in that: You can't copy someone else's spirituality. What those prayer warriors were doing was great because it came directly out of their fellowship with God. But what the other people were doing only came out of watching someone else.

God never created you to be like anyone else. He only makes originals. God wants you to operate out of your own heart. He wants you to listen for the cues the Holy Spirit is giving you personally.

Cues? Yes, cues! Subtle signals and hints. Quiet inner suggestions. God is giving His people cues all the time. But most people miss them because they're looking for the wrong thing. They're looking for something spectacular. They want goose pimples and a great revelation to get them started praying.

But the Holy Spirit doesn't usually operate like that. What He does is send you cues, and if you're not looking in the right place, you'll miss them.

Have you ever been driving along in your car and someone that you haven't thought of in years suddenly crosses your mind? Then two weeks later, you hear they were in a car accident and are laid up in the hospital. You go see them and say, "Isn't it strange? I was just thinking about you two weeks ago."

Do you know what you did? You missed your cue. The Holy Spirit is inside you. Do you think He brought that person to your mind so you could just think about them? No, He wanted you to pray!

If you'll learn to respond to those cues and yield to that force, it will get bigger and bigger. He'll give you more and more people to pray about. He'll even start giving you cues to pray for people you don't know.

That happened to me a few years ago. All summer long, I prayed for a man I'd never heard of. The Holy Spirit just caused his name to come up inside me. It was "Guy Hunter." When I prayed for him, I could see him crouched down in some sort of a box. The heat was coming down on that box and he was about to suffocate. So I prayed Psalm 91 over him fervently. I prayed the protection of God over him.

One morning, just after the war with Iraq had begun, I turned on the television and heard the newscasters talking about the prisoners of war who had been taken captive. One of the pilots mentioned was Guy Hunter!

I just said, "Glory to God!" because I knew he'd be all right. I'd been praying for him all summer. You see, the Holy Spirit doesn't want you to be praying about things after they've already happened. He wants to show you things to come so you can get to them with the power of God before they get to you.

That's supernatural praying. It is what God wants for His people. It's not the kind of praying where you say, "Let me see now, where's my prayer list? What Word can I pray over this situation?"

Praying like this involves a supernatural move of God. But remember, that move doesn't necessarily start with lightning bolts or great revelations. It begins with those quiet little cues from the Holy Spirit.

So start listening for those cues. Pray from your heart. Let the Holy Spirit lead. When He gives you His Word about the outcome of a situation, pray it fervently and don't let it go. And above all, keep your faith constantly in gear.

Those are the elements that will bring the power of God to bear in a situation. Those are the elements that will take you into supernatural prayer. Believe me, in the emergency hours ahead, that kind of prayer is not just an option. It's the only thing strong enough to see us through.

Chapter 8

The Power of Pleasing the Father

*Gloria
Copeland*

"That ye might be filled with the knowledge of [God's] will in all wisdom and spiritual understanding; That ye might walk worthy of the Lord unto all pleasing, being fruitful in every good work, and increasing in the knowledge of God; Strengthened with all might, according to his glorious power."

— COLOSSIANS 1:9-11

Right now I'm hungrier for God than I have ever been in my life. I'm hungry to know Him better. I'm hungry for a greater manifestation of His presence. I'm hungry for Jesus to be fully formed in me.

I'm not alone in that desire. Far from it. Everywhere I go, I see believers who are desiring more of God. I meet Christians whose hearts are crying out to be changed and filled with greater degrees of the glory of God.

A sense of urgency has been implanted in our spirit by the Spirit of God because the end of this age is very near. Time is running out and God is fulfilling His plan in us. He is preparing for Himself a glorious Church without spot or wrinkle. He is raising up a people who will walk in the things He has prepared for them.

God is bringing forth a multitude of believers who will fulfill the divine destiny prepared for them since the beginning of time. That destiny is defined clearly in Romans 8:29: *"For those whom [God] foreknew—of whom He was aware and loved beforehand—He also destined from the beginning (foreordaining them) to be molded into the image of His Son [and share inwardly His likeness], that He might become the firstborn among many brethren"* (AMP).

Our destiny as believers is to grow up in Jesus. It's to be fully conformed to His image which was placed within us the moment we were born again.

It's a staggering thought that you and I could ever truly be transformed into that divine image. It seems almost impossible that we could be like Jesus. But God says we can be. In fact, the Bible says He has equipped us with everything necessary so that we might continue growing and developing:

> **Until we all attain oneness in the faith and in the comprehension of the full and accurate knowledge of the Son of God; that [we might arrive] at really mature manhood—the completeness of personality which is nothing less than the standard height of Christ's own perfection—the measure of the stature of the fullness of the Christ, and the completeness found in Him** (Ephesians 4:13, AMP).

If anyone other than the Spirit of God had written that, I wouldn't be able to believe it. But the Spirit of God did write it! So as amazing as it seems, we must simply believe that He has the ability to conform us to Jesus so completely that we *"become a body wholly filled and flooded with God Himself!"* (Ephesians 3:19, AMP).

We Must Do Our Part

Not only is God able to do that, it is His will for us. It is His end-time plan. But whether or not that divine plan will come to pass in our own individual lives is up to us. If we want to be a part of God's plan, we must do our part of God's plan.

That's how it has always been. In Genesis 18:19, God said of Abraham: *"For I know him, that he will command his children and his household after him, and they shall keep the way of the Lord, to do justice and judgment; that the Lord may bring upon Abraham that which he hath spoken of him."*

Abraham's part was to cooperate with the Lord. If Abraham didn't do that—if he didn't obey what God told him to do—God couldn't fulfill His promise to make Abraham a father of many nations, even though it was His will.

The same is true for us today. It is God's will that we be conformed to the image of Jesus. It is His will to manifest Himself in our lives just as He manifested

Himself through Jesus' life. But He cannot do it until we do our part.

Our part is simply this: to walk pleasing before Him—to think His thoughts, to speak His words. In other words, to walk in His ways.

If we want to fulfill our divine destiny and enjoy the fullness of the power of God in our lives, we must make a decision and a determination to stop living to please ourselves and start living every moment of every day to please the Father. We must walk out the prayer the Apostle Paul prayed for the Colossians: *"That ye might be filled with the knowledge of [God's] will in all wisdom and spiritual understanding; That ye might walk worthy of the Lord unto all pleasing, being fruitful in every good work, and increasing in the knowledge of God; Strengthened with all might, according to his glorious power"* (Colossians 1:9-11).

Notice that verse connects pleasing the Lord with the manifestation of God's glorious power. It says they come together.

The life of Jesus was proof. He said, *"He that sent me is with me: the Father hath not left me alone; for I do always those things that please him"* (John 8:29).

We talk a lot about the fact that God will never leave us nor forsake us. And it's true, He is always with us. But we have to admit, His power is not always in manifestation.

In Jesus' life, however, God's power was constantly in manifestation. Every moment of every hour of every day, Jesus walked in the measureless, manifested power and presence of God because He always did those things that pleased the Father.

I am able to do nothing from Myself—independently, of My own accord—but as I am taught by God and as I get His orders. [I decide as I am bidden to decide. As the voice comes to Me, so I give decision.] Even as I hear, I judge and My judgment is right (just, righteous), because I do not seek or consult My own will—I have no desire to do what is pleasing to Myself, My own aim, My own purpose—but only the will and pleasure of the Father Who sent Me (John 5:30, AMP).

"And He Who sent Me is ever with Me; My Father has not left Me alone, for I always do what pleases Him" (John 8:29, AMP).

God was able to say of Him, *"Thou art my beloved Son, in whom I am well pleased"* (Mark 1:11).

Light...Not Twilight!

There's no reason why we as believers can't please God as much as Jesus did. We have a reborn spirit made in His image. We've been given His righteousness. We've been filled with the same Holy Spirit. We have all the capacity that Jesus had in the earth to be just like Him and to do the works that He did because He lives in us. The Scripture says, *"Christ in you, the hope of glory"* (Colossians 1:27).

He was dedicated. He was totally sold out to God. He was without sin. The Bible tells us many times He ministered to the multitudes all day and then prayed all night, yet Jesus had a flesh and blood body just like yours and mine. He enjoyed a good night's sleep just as much as we do. So there was an element of crucifying the flesh involved in giving up that sleep and doing what pleased God. He had to say no to His flesh and yes to the Father.

"Well, Gloria, I know Jesus did that, but God doesn't expect that kind of self-sacrifice from us."

Yes, He does. First Peter 4:1-3 says:

So, since Christ suffered in the flesh [for us, for you], arm your-selves with the same thought and purpose [patiently to suffer rather than fail to please God]. For who-ever has suffered in the flesh [having the mind of Christ] has done with [intentional] sin—has stopped pleas-ing himself and the world, and pleases God. So that he can no longer spend the rest of his natural life living by [his] human appetites and desires, but [he lives] for what God wills. For the time that is past already

suffices for doing what the Gentiles like to do (AMP).

It's time for the Church to stop living as gentiles (or sinners) do! It's time for the Church to live as God says, regardless of what the world around us is doing. Just because the morals of the world slip doesn't mean the morals in the Church should slip.

It doesn't matter how dark this world gets, we are to be the light of this world. Not the twilight of the world—the light!

We need to fight against compromise by arming ourselves with the commitment to suffer in the flesh rather than fail to please God. To suffer in the flesh doesn't mean to bear sickness and poverty without complaining. Jesus already bore sickness and poverty for us along with every other curse of the law so that we can be free from those things. We are expected to resist that curse in Jesus' Name.

Suffering in the flesh is making your flesh do something it doesn't want to do. It's dedicating yourself to do what's pleasing to God even when it causes your flesh discomfort.

When you're ready to do that, you'll go beyond just "not sinning" and into a life that's pleasing to God. You'll be ready to lay down those things that you enjoy, things that aren't necessarily bad in themselves, yet they are hindering your walk with God.

If you want to walk in the best God has for you, those are the kinds of sacrifices you must make, for Jesus said: *"He who does not take up his cross and follow Me [that is, cleave steadfastly to Me, conforming wholly to My example in living and if need be in dying also] is not worthy of Me. Whoever finds his [lower] life will lose [the higher life], and whosoever loses his [lower] life on My account will find [the higher life]"* (Matthew 10:38-39, AMP).

If you could see what God has for you in the higher life, you would immediately let go of the mundane things of the world. You would drop that junk so fast you wouldn't even know which way it went. But you're not going to be able to see it and then make your decision.

You have to step into that higher life by faith. You have to lay down your life because the Word says to do it. Then and only then will you discover the wonders that are waiting on the other side of your obedience.

I'm sure Enoch didn't know what the higher life held for him. He probably had no idea that he'd be the first man ever raptured. But he was. Hebrews 11:5 says, *"By faith Enoch was translated that he should not see death...for before his translation he had this testimony, that he pleased God."*

Righteousness and Holiness: Two Different Things

How do you develop the spiritual strength to do the things that please the Father rather than the things that please yourself? First and foremost by spending time in the Word and in prayer. When the power of God was being displayed through the early apostles in great signs and wonders, that's what they were doing. They were giving themselves *"continually to prayer, and to the ministry of the word"* (Acts 6:4).

Romans 8:5 says it this way: *"For they that are after the flesh do mind the things of the flesh; but they that are after the Spirit the things of the Spirit."* That is the matter in a nutshell. If you want to grow physically and build big muscles, you have to spend time lifting weights and doing physical things to build those muscles. If you want to grow spiritually, you will have to spend time doing spiritual things.

As you spend time fellowshiping with God in His Word, by the power of that Word the Holy Spirit will separate you not only from sin, but also from the unnecessary things of life. He will impart to you the spiritual might and grace you need to obey the instructions in Ephesians 4:22-24:

> Strip yourselves of your former nature—put off and discard your old unrenewed self—which characterized your previous manner of life and becomes corrupt through lusts and desires that spring from delusion; And be constantly renewed in the spirit of your mind—having a fresh mental and spiritual attitude;

And put on the new nature (the regenerate self) created in God's image, (Godlike) in true righteousness and holiness (AMP).

That verse tells us that righteousness and holiness are two different things. Righteousness is the right-standing with God you gained when you were born again. The only thing you did to be made righteous was to make Jesus Christ the Lord of your life.

Holiness, however, is another matter. You are not made holy. Holiness is the result of your choices. It's what you do with your time and your actions. It's your conduct. It comes when you make a decision of your will to live according to the precepts of the Lord. In short, holiness is doing those things that please the Father.

To be holy is to be *"sanctified, and meet for the master's use"* (2 Timothy 2:21). *Sanctified* means "set apart." Set apart from what? From the world! God wants us to be so caught up in spiritual things that we lose interest in carnal activities and pursue Him with all our heart.

He doesn't want us to simply obey a set of rules because it's the "right thing to do." That's law instead of spirit. God wants us to live holy lives because we have a heart-felt desire to please Him. When we spend time with the Lord, we want to do the things that please Him. Our desire is for spiritual things, not the things of the flesh. It shouldn't be a "head thing" but a "heart thing." Time with Him separates us to Him. He wants us to love Him so much that we want to be wholly dedicated to Him!

And He doesn't want us to consider such holiness as something out of the ordinary. He wants us to take the attitude of the Apostle Paul, who said to the believers at Rome: *"I beseech you therefore, brethren, by the mercies of God, that ye present your bodies a living sacrifice, holy, acceptable unto God, which is your reasonable service. And be not conformed to this world: but be ye transformed by the renewing of your mind, that ye may prove what is that good, and acceptable, and perfect, will of God"* (Romans 12:1-2).

Being wholly dedicated to God is your reasonable service. It's not something above and beyond the call of duty. It's not something that is just expected of preachers and ministers. God expects us all to live holy. He says, *"Be ye holy; for I am holy"* (1 Peter 1:16).

Certainly such a life will require us to make some sacrifices. It will cause us to suffer in the flesh at times. But it will be worth it. For *"the sufferings of this present time are not worthy to be compared with the glory which shall be revealed in us"* (Romans 8:18).

When you see the power and glory of God start to flow in greater measure through you, you won't regret you made those sacrifices; you'll be glad! When you lay hands on a crippled person and see him raised instantly out of a wheelchair, you'll be glad you turned down that carnal movie your friends were going to see. You'll be glad that you gave up those hours of sleep so you could spend extra time in the Word and in prayer.

When you speak in the Name of Jesus to someone in bondage and the devil instantly flees and they go free, you won't be wishing you'd spent more time pleasing yourself; you'll be thanking God you chose to please Him instead.

You may think I'm being overly dramatic, but I'm not. Those things are going to happen—not just at the hands of famous preachers and full-time ministers, but at the hands of everyday believers. We've already started to see it. But we're just on the edge of what's coming. We haven't seen anything yet!

The prophets of God are telling us that we are about to see the greatest outpouring of God's power this earth has ever known. It's been said that if we were told all that's about to happen, we would not be able to believe it because the magnitude of it is so great.

Glory to God, we are about to see multitudes of Christians put aside the distractions of this age and rise up in the strength of God Himself! We are about to see believers conformed to the image of Jesus! We are about to see the Church God has always dreamed of—a Church holy and without blemish!

Determine in your heart to be a part of it all. Make up your mind that you won't be sidelined by doing petty things that please yourself. Dedicate yourself to live wholly pleasing to the Father and get ready for a life of power!

The Way of the Winner—Part 2

"[God] giveth power to the faint; and to them that have no might he increaseth strength…. They that wait upon the Lord shall renew their strength; they shall mount up with wings as eagles; they shall run, and not be weary; and they shall walk, and not faint."
— ISAIAH 40:29, 31

Mac Hammond

Imagine yourself stepping into the winner's circle...head high...arms raised in victory. Imagine yourself shouting in triumph with the Apostle Paul, "I've fought the good fight! I've run my race! I've finished my course!" It's a thrilling thought, isn't it?

But let me tell you something. It's meant to be more than a passing thought. It's your destiny in Christ Jesus.

God made you to be a winner. He created you to win—and win big! To *"press toward the mark for the prize of the high calling of God in Christ Jesus"* (Philippians 3:14).

The Way of the Loser

But let's be honest. A great many born-again "winners" are living like losers these days. Good, Christian people—people who love God and want His will for their lives—are failing in their relationships, in their finances and in their careers. And the primary reason is this: They aren't following the victory prescription Paul gave us in Philippians 3. They aren't pressing (straining, expending maximum effort) toward the mark.

Why aren't they? At the most basic level, it's because they don't believe it will do them any good. They don't believe they can win.

You see, in a very real sense, it takes faith to press successfully. You have to truly believe that what you're doing is going to produce the desired result, or you'll never press long enough, hard enough or consistently enough to arrive at the goal.

The secret to developing that kind of faith can be found in Hebrews 11:1. It says, *"Faith is the substance of things hoped for."* So in reality, faith begins with hope!

But instead of having hope, or a positive expectation, many people today have developed exactly the opposite—a negative expectancy, which is leading them down the way of the loser. I've seen it happen many times. Someone who needs healing, for example, might come forward for prayer. If his healing doesn't manifest itself instantly, he may go away disappointed. His original hope or expectancy has been frustrated. That, by the way, is precisely how Webster's defines *disappointment*: "the frustration of expectancy."

Later he hears a little more of the Word, and hope begins to rise again. Once again his healing doesn't manifest immediately, and once more he suffers disappointment. If that happens repeatedly, he can eventually develop a strong negative expectancy concerning healing.

It's a deadly cycle that begins with disappointment, moves to discouragement and, if left unchecked, will ultimately lead to despair.

That's what happened to Elijah. According to 1 Kings 18, he defeated over 400 prophets of Baal on Mount Carmel. Fire rained down, the prophets of Baal were put to the sword and God was greatly magnified. It was a mighty victory over idolatry in Israel.

Elijah must have thought, *Surely now this nation and its leadership will repent and turn from Baal worship.* Yet he was shattered by disappointment when Queen Jezebel's only response was to threaten to have him killed.

It wasn't the fear of death that sent the prophet running for the hills. He had just faced down more than 400 demonic sorcerers. No, it was disappointment that took the wind out of his sails—disappointment that a magnificent display of God's power had failed to move the queen. To Elijah's dismay, the nation continued in idolatry in spite of the great miracle.

That shattering disappointment quickly took him on to discouragement and dark despair. As a result, he fled to the wilderness, sat down in a cave and asked to die.

I can't tell you how many times people have sat across from my desk and said, "I don't have anything to live for." Imagine that! Born-again, Spirit-filled people who don't want to live because they've walked in the way of the loser. They've moved from disappointment to discouragement to despair, and now they want to curl up and die.

Dealing With the Force of Disappointment

Obviously, if you're going to avoid the way of the loser and walk in the way of the winner, it's crucial that you deal properly with disappointment. Philippians 3, our foundational passage of Scripture concerning pressing toward the mark of the high calling of God, shows us how. There in verse 13, Paul says you must forget *"those things which are behind."*

The quickest way to get into discouragement and despair is to focus on past disappointments. So don't do it! Don't dwell on the disappointment you felt when you didn't get that promotion. Don't keep mentally rehearsing those words of rejection that were spoken to you. Those memories will put you on the fast track to despair, deception or worse.

Even thoughts about the good things in the past can trip you up. They can lead you to feel disappointment about your current situation if it's not quite as bright as in days gone by.

Good or bad, you must leave the past behind. So, every time memories of disappointments arise in your consciousness (the Bible calls them "vain imaginations"), cast them down.

Releasing the Power of God Through Service

Once the past is safely behind you, you're ready to meet the challenges that stand between you and the winner's circle. Those challenges could be financial. They could be physical. They could involve relationships. Whatever they are, those challenges can be won with the power of God. Isaiah 40:29, 31 tells us what we must do for that power to be released in our lives. It says:

> He [God] giveth power to the faint; and to them that have no might he increaseth strength...They that

wait upon the Lord shall renew their strength; they shall mount up with wings as eagles; they shall run, and not be weary; and they shall walk, and not faint.

The words "wait upon" as used in that scripture actually refer to a servant waiting on his master's needs. In other words, as we wait upon God's needs and purposes in the earth, as we serve Him expecting Him to empower us, He'll release the might we need to be winners in every circumstance.

Yes, I said every circumstance! Pressing toward the mark of servanthood can turn even the bleakest of situations around 180 degrees.

Job proved that. He had big problems. No matter how desperate your circumstances, you're probably not as bad off as he was. If you'll read the book of Job, you'll see that for some 41 chapters, Job tried to get God to heal him. He was completely focused on his own need the entire time. He clearly loved God and God clearly loved him. Yet he could not seem to figure out how to get God's divine provision and power operating on his behalf.

Then in chapter 42, Job finally turned his focus outward. He prayed for his friends and began to serve the needs of others rather than focusing on his own. When he did, the power of God was immediately released in his circumstances. Not only was he healed, he ended up twice as wealthy as he had previously been.

In your life, just as in Job's, the power of God will be released when you orient your life toward the mark of service to others. It will heal you, restore you and provide for your every need. In fact, as you press toward the mark of servanthood, the power of God will open doors of opportunity you never dreamed existed. He'll exalt you and give you visibility and influence in your community.

He'll keep on propelling you toward your dream until one day you'll look around and find that you've arrived at the high calling of God for your life. The place of fulfillment. The place of meaning and purpose. The place of blessing. You'll find you've made it to the winner's circle, at last!

Life Forces: Your Inside Answer to Outside Pressure

Kenneth Copeland

Chapter 10

"Keep thy heart with all diligence; for out of it are the issues of life."

— Proverbs 4:23

The pressure is on. There's no question about it. We have more to do these days, and less time to do it in, than ever before.

Things, both in the natural world and in the world of the spirit, are moving at a rapid-fire pace. It's exhilarating—and it can also be draining. In fact, if you don't learn how to handle the pressure, it can drain you completely dry.

I know, because at one time in my life I let it happen to me. I felt like I was the most tired man in the world back then. I was so tired that no amount of rest would help. I went to bed tired and I woke up tired. Every bone in my body ached. At times, Gloria had to physically help me out of bed.

I felt much like the Apostle Paul must have felt when he wrote in 2 Corinthians 1:8: *"For we would not, brethren, have you ignorant of our trouble...that we were pressed out of measure, above strength, insomuch that we despaired even of life."*

At that time in his ministry, Paul was under so much pressure he despaired of life. That's what I did too. I got to the point where I wasn't even fighting to live anymore. I went to God and said, "I've had all this I can stand. I just want to come on home now."

What causes that kind of devastating fatigue? It took me a long time to find out, but when I did, I realized it was really very simple. My life force was being drained out. I was giving out more spiritual strength than I was putting back into myself. As a result, I developed a spiritual deficit that very nearly killed me.

Let me give you a word of warning. Don't believe the old adage that says what you don't know won't hurt you. God's Word says just the opposite. *"My people are destroyed for lack of knowledge"* (Hosea 4:6). In the spirit realm, what you don't know can kill you.

Guard Your Generator

Most people don't know, for example, where their life force resides. They don't know their spirits are the generators that provide energy for everything they do. So they fail to take care of those generators. They overload them and neglect them until they "burn out."

Let me illustrate. Say you have a 100-watt generator and you start plugging 10-watt bulbs into the circuit that generator supplies. You can put in 10 bulbs and they'll all burn brightly. Your generator will be running at full capacity, pulling all the load it's made to pull.

When you put bulb number 11 on line, the whole string will dim a little. If you put in a 12th bulb, they'll dim a little more. Put in 13, and you'll see smoke coming out of that generator. It will burn out because it's not equipped to produce 130 watts.

What happens then? All the lights go out. Not just the three extras you put in—all of them go out. The overload knocks out the whole string.

That's what is happening to many dedicated believers today. They're so busy ministering, so busy working *for* God instead of *with* God, they're overloading their spiritual generators. They're putting out more than they're putting in.

Proverbs 4:23 warns us against such careless treatment of our spirits. It says, *"Keep thy heart [or spirit] with all diligence; for out of it are the issues [or forces] of life."* Most people don't understand the importance of obeying that verse. They think if they eat right and rest and exercise, they'll have all the strength they need. But they're wrong. The real strength for living, the force that literally keeps the body alive, comes from the spirit man.

Your body has to have strength and life from your spirit being or it can't function.

When your spirit is strong, you can sleep a few hours, eat a good healthy meal, work out a little and you're ready to go again. But when your spirit is weak, it doesn't matter how many hours you sleep or how many vegetables you eat, you just can't seem to get on top of things.

The Answer Is Inside

When you're suffering from that kind of weakness, you need to follow Paul's example. He wrote, *"Though our outward man perish, yet the inward man is renewed day by day"* (2 Corinthians 4:16). In spite of all the pressure Paul was under, in spite of the fact that he had despaired of life, he found the strength not just to go on, but to go on in victory.

Where did he find that strength? In his inward man! In his own reborn spirit!

It doesn't matter how tired you are. It doesn't matter how depressed you feel. It doesn't even matter if you feel like you've been dragged through a knothole backward and you're so stressed out you can't take one more step. The answer to your situation is not "out there" somewhere. The answer is inside you.

Look again at what Paul said in 2 Corinthians 1:8-9 about his predicament: *"We were pressed out of measure, above strength, insomuch that we despaired even of life: But we had the sentence of death in ourselves."* If you'll look up the Greek word translated *sentence* in that last phrase, you'll find the better translation is the word "answer."

Now, actually a sentence is an answer. When someone robs a bank and they're sentenced to 10 years in prison, that 10 years is the legal answer to their crime. Keep that in mind when you read these verses and you'll realize how truly powerful they are.

We were pressed out of measure...insomuch that we despaired even of life: But we had the sentence [or answer] of death in ourselves.

When the pressure is so great it's about to kill you, where do you look for the answer? Inside your own reborn, Holy Ghost-filled spirit!

Your deliverance is inside you because that's where the Holy Spirit is. Your help is inside you because that's where your Helper is. The joy, the strength, the love...everything you've been looking for is right there inside your spirit.

Fast and Feast

"Oh, but Brother Copeland, my spirit hasn't been in very good shape lately. I've been too tired to read my Bible or go to church. All I've had the energy to do is lie around and watch television." Well then, you're in trouble.

To get out of that trouble, start feeding the man of faith on the inside of you. Set aside some of the physical food you've been chewing on and sink your spiritual teeth into the Word of God.

Take a day or two to fast in your body and feast in your spirit!

Fasting helps give your spirit man a rest. All the physical operations of the body drain energy from the spirit. You have many involuntary physical functions, for example, that go to work every time you eat a meal. Those functions take a toll on the spirit. They drain your generator. When you fast, you give your spirit a break.

That's why it's good every once in a while to fast a few meals and just be quiet. Don't do anything. Don't put any pressure on. Just be still. Go get back in bed and turn your tapes on, read your Bible for a few hours and sip a little fruit juice.

Shut down all the physical functions you can and feed on the Word. You don't even have to pray. Just be still for a while and know that God is God. Let the Word rejuvenate your spirit man. When you do pray during that time, pray in the spirit. Relax in God's presence.

There's an old religious cliché that used to be especially popular among ministers. "We're just going to burn ourselves out for God," they'd say. That's not what God wants. That's what the devil wants! He would love to see you just work yourself until you "burn out" and die. He'd kick up his heels at your funeral!

Don't give him that opportunity. Take the time to feed your inner man so you won't "burn out." Keep feeding your spirit until you increase your strength. Burn brighter and stronger every year.

Be transformed from glory to glory by *"beholding as in a glass the glory of the Lord"* (2 Corinthians 3:18). Increase the wattage of your spiritual generator by spending time focusing on the Lord. Take your focus off the things of the world and look at Him. Begin to work with Him instead of just for Him.

Not Just in Heaven—In You!

Where must you look to see Jesus? First, in the Word. And second, in your own spirit.

That second place is where most of us have trouble. We can see Jesus as great and magnificent in the Word of God. We can envision Him sitting grandly in heaven at the right hand of the Father. But we haven't developed our ability to see Him living inside us.

You must have that ability to survive the pressure in these last days. You'll need to be able to see Jesus within you just as clearly as you can see Him in the Word. You'll have to know—not just with your brain but with every fiber of your being— that He Who is within you is greater than he that is in the world.

Never forget this: Once you truly see that the very Spirit and power of Jesus reside on the inside of you, nothing—no amount of debt, no disease, no problem of ANY kind—will be able to defeat you. When your inner image of the Jesus Who lives in you becomes bigger than your image of the problems around you, you'll conquer any challenge the devil brings your way.

So get to work on that inner image. Begin to look inside yourself and say, "I am the righteousness of God. I have fellowship with my heavenly Father. I do walk with Him hand in hand, and Jesus Christ is my blood Brother. Through Him, I have an eternal blood covenant with Almighty God."

I know you're facing needs. I know you're facing difficulties. But I also know that 2 Peter 1:3 says God has already given you *"all things that pertain unto life and godliness, through the knowledge of [Jesus]."* Once you develop that inner knowledge of Him, those needs will be met and those difficulties overcome.

The answer to everything is inside you right now. Everything you'll ever need is in your spirit. All the money...all the health... all the strength...all the wisdom...all of it is in you because that's where Jesus is!

We have this treasure in earthen vessels, Paul says, "that the excellency of the power may be of God, and not of us" (2 Corinthians 4:7).

Pressure?...What Pressure?

I'm not telling you there won't be trouble on the outside. Certainly there will be trouble. As a matter of fact, Paul said he

was troubled by circumstances on every side...
but on the inside he was not distressed.

> **We are troubled on every side,
> yet not distressed; we are perplexed,
> but not in despair; Persecuted, but
> not forsaken; cast down, but not
> destroyed (2 Corinthians 4:8-9).**

Paul fixed his attention not on external
circumstances, but on his inner man because
that's where the excellency of God's power
is. "We're perplexed," he said. The Greek
word translated *perplexed* means "to be
cornered by the circumstances." *"But we're
not in despair."* In other words, even when
it looks as if there's no way out, I can find
a way out if I look on the inside.

Persecuted, but not forsaken. If I'm
persecuted on the outside, how do I know
God hasn't forsaken me? Because when I
look on the inside, I can see Jesus saying,
"I'll never leave you nor forsake you, even
to the ends of the earth."

Perplexed...persecuted...cast down. There's
no doubt about it, Paul was under more
pressure than most of us today will ever

experience. But he handled it...and so can you if you'll do these three things:

1. Remember where the pressure is coming from. (The outside!) And remember where your life force comes from. (The inside!)

2. Stop running on a spiritual deficit. Take time to feed your inner man with the Word of God. Fast your body if necessary and feast your spirit on the Word so your inner man can get stronger more quickly.

3. Focus on Jesus inside you until your inner picture of Him is bigger than the outside situations you're facing.

If you'll build up your spirit man in those three ways, when pressure comes it won't affect you like it used to. Problems that once knocked you flat won't even bother you anymore.

Think about it. A 5-foot, 140-pound bully who scared you silly when you were in the second grade couldn't even make you blink now that you're 6 feet tall. You've grown. You're stronger now. That second-grade bully isn't a threat anymore.

That's what happened to Paul. He grew! He kept feeding on the Word until the image of Jesus within him grew bigger than the pressures around him. He grew up so much that just a few years after he wrote about being *"pressed out of measure, above strength, insomuch that we despaired even of life"* he wrote, *"I have learned, in whatsoever state I am, therewith to be content. I can do all things through Christ which strengtheneth me"* (2 Corinthians 1:8; Philippians 4:11, 13).

Don't let the bullies get you down. Just keep feeding your spirit man on the Word. Get strong on the inside. One of these days, when the circumstances are putting the squeeze on you and someone asks how you handle the pressure, you'll look at them with surprise and say, "Pressure?...What pressure?"

Chapter 11

Doors No Man Can Shut!

Jerry Savelle

"A man's gift maketh room for him, and bringeth him before great men."

— PROVERBS 18:16

"Brother, please join us at the head table."

"Sister, here is a financial gift to get your project started. Please let us know if there's anything else we can do to help."

"I don't know why the board decided to consider such a low offer, but we have voted to sell you the land."

Support. Endorsements. Doors opened before you that once seemed impossibly slammed shut and locked.

No, I'm not talking about something that belongs to the rich and famous. What I am describing is the heritage of every believer—an essential element for completing the work God has for the Body of Christ to do in these last days.

It's called walking in the favor of God. And quite frankly, it's the only way to live.

Bring You Before Great Men

Let me give you an example of how God's favor supernaturally opened a door for me early in my ministry.

For the first three years I was in the ministry, I worked for Kenneth Copeland. During that time, he talked a lot about what a blessing Kenneth Hagin had been to him. There were times when we were in the same room with Brother Hagin—I'd be standing right next to Brother Copeland as he talked to Brother Hagin—but I never met the man! I was close enough to touch him, but never once was I introduced! I wanted to nudge Brother Copeland and whisper, "Tell him I'm your servant. Please introduce me to this man." But I didn't. The Bible says, *"A man's gift maketh room for him, and bringeth him before great men"* (Proverbs 18:16). So I waited until God opened that door for me.

And He did—in a spectacular way. The first time I actually met Brother Hagin was at the first Believers' Convention Kenneth Copeland Ministries conducted. The speakers were Charles Capps, Kenneth E. Hagin, Kenneth and Gloria Copeland...and me. I was to speak just before Brother Hagin.

When I started to preach, a strong anointing came over the entire congregation. In fact, right in the middle of my sermon, a lady got up out of a wheelchair and began walking. The Anointing of God was so strong that she received her healing while I was preaching! Still, I was conscious of not wanting to run over into Brother Hagin's time, so when my time was up, although the anointing was still there, I stopped and said, "Well, my time is up. I'm going to turn the service over to Brother Hagin."

But Brother Hagin stood up and said, "I don't need any practice preaching. I know when the anointing is present. Keep preaching, boy."

So I preached a little more, but I was still concerned about taking his time. Finally, I shut it off again and sat down. I said to Brother Hagin, "Well, Brother Hagin, my time's up. It's your time now."

After the service—now remember, this was the first time I'd ever met Brother Hagin— he walked up to me and said, "God told me there are some young men coming on the scene that will do more than we've been able to do in the past." And then he said, "You are one of those men, and I want you to preach in my campmeeting this year."

Well, that's not bad! The first time you meet Kenneth E. Hagin he asks you to preach in his convention! I call that favor. I didn't make that door open. Kenneth Copeland didn't make that door open. God opened it with His divine favor. And since that time, I've had the privilege of preaching with whom I consider to be some of the greatest men and women of God in our generation. But I've never once had to make it happen. Those doors opened because I have always confessed and believed that I'm walking in the favor of God.

Provided With Advantages

"But, Brother Jerry," you may be asking, "just what is favor? I want to walk in the favor of God, but how will I know if I am or not? And anyway, I'm not a preacher. How is walking in God's favor going to open doors for me? How is the favor of God going to benefit me in my everyday Christian life?"

Well, thank God, divine favor is not just for preachers! It's for every child of God who will claim it by faith. Why? Because favor is by God's grace. It's a free gift.

What is grace? The definition of *grace* that I like best is "the ability of God coming on you to do what you can't do for yourself." When Paul says, *"By grace ye are saved"* (Ephesians 2:5), he means that God's grace had to do something in us that we couldn't do for ourselves. I couldn't save myself. It took grace. It took God's ability to do in me what I couldn't do in myself.

Secondly, grace is often defined as unmerited favor. That brings us to the definition of favor. My dictionary defines *favor* as "to support, to endorse, to assist, to make easier, to provide with advantages and to show special privileges." So when you're walking in the favor of God, you can expect to be supported, endorsed, assisted, to have things made easier for you, to be provided with advantages and shown special privileges.

Sounds like a great way to live, doesn't it? Are you living that way in your everyday Christian life? If not, it may be that you haven't fully realized the wonderful benefits—your birthright as a believer—because of what Jesus did for you at Calvary. Psalm 103:2 says, *"Bless the Lord, O my soul, and forget not all his benefits."* There are a number of benefits of walking in the favor of God.

Increased Assets

One of them is financial abundance. Isaiah 60:5 says when God's favor is bestowed on you, *"the forces of the Gentiles shall come unto thee."* In Hebrew, the word translated *forces* means "wealth." In fact, the *New International Version* says, *"To you the riches of the nations will come."* Riches, hallelujah! Favor produces wealth.

According to the Bible, one of the ways the wealth that favor produces will be manifest is in the area of real estate (Deuteronomy 8:7-9, 33:23). Do you need some real estate? Then lay hold of these promises. That's what I did recently, and God gave me special favor in the purchase of a large plot of land.

Title Deed to a Piece of the Planet

You need God's favor when you're buying real estate, not only because God will see to it that you get a better price, but because when a Christian has the title deed to a piece of land, it enforces the devil's defeat in the spirit realm. Brother Oral Roberts taught me that years ago.

One day he asked me, "Jerry, do you know why it seems that every demon in hell fights churches when they try to buy property?"

"No," I said. But I was anxious to hear what Oral Roberts had to say about it.

He said, "It's because the devil thinks he owns the planet. But when a member of the Body of Christ purchases real estate, he gets the title deed to a piece of the planet.

And that reminds the devil that *'The earth is the Lord's, and the fulness thereof'* (Psalm 24:1). It enforces the fact in the spirit realm that the devil doesn't own the planet like he thinks he does!"

The Least Likely to Succeed

Not only does walking in the favor of God bring wealth and increased assets, but God's favor will bring you promotion and recognition even in situations where you seem the least likely to receive them.

When Joseph was thrown into prison after being falsely accused by Potiphar's wife, it must have seemed as if he would have been the last man in that prison who would receive special notice from the warden.

But the Lord was with Joseph, and showed him mercy, and gave him favour in the sight of the keeper of the prison. And the keeper of the prison committed to Joseph's hand all the prisoners that were in the prison; and whatsoever they did there, he was the doer of it. The

> keeper of the prison looked not to
> any thing that was under his hand;
> because the Lord was with him, and
> that which he did, the Lord made it
> to prosper (Genesis 39:21-23).

Talk about promotion! From Hebrew
slave accused of making improper advances
toward the wife of a prominent Egyptian to
assistant warden—all because Joseph
walked in the favor of God. And, of course,
Joseph's promotion didn't stop there. It was
through God's favor that he was later
brought to the attention of Pharaoh and
was promoted to be a ruler over Egypt.
God's favor opened the prison door for
Joseph even though, as a foreigner and a
slave, he seemed the least likely man in all
of Egypt to be promoted.

Even if you've been voted the member
of your family "least likely to succeed," the
favor of God will bring you recognition
and promotion. In 1 Samuel 16, God sent
the prophet Samuel to Jesse in Bethlehem to
anoint one of his sons as king over Israel.
Samuel didn't know which one God had
chosen, so he had Jesse line up all his sons,

and he went down the line looking at each one. But God said no to all of them.

Then Samuel asked Jesse whether all his children were there, and Jesse said, "Well, no, there's one more—the youngest—but he's out herding sheep."

Samuel then told Jesse, *"Send for him, for we will not sit down to eat until he is here"* (verse 11, AMP).

So Jesse sent for David, and when he came in, *"The Lord said [to Samuel], Arise, anoint him; this is he. Then Samuel took the horn of oil, and anointed David...and the Spirit of the Lord came mightily upon David from that day forward"* (verses 12-13, AMP).

The Spirit of the Lord came upon him mightily from that day forward! That's the favor of God. David's family didn't think he was fit for much more than herding sheep. But by the favor of God he was recognized and promoted to be king over Israel, and the earthly ancestor of the Messiah—the good Shepherd Who gives *"his life for the sheep"* (John 10:11) and the door by Whom *"if any man enter in, he shall be saved"* (John 10:9).

This same shepherd boy who was promoted through God's favor to be king over His people, later wrote that we are compassed about by the favor of God (Psalm 5:12). One translation says we're "surrounded" by it. That's the way, as believers, we ought to be living every day— conscious of being surrounded by God's favor, and by His grace.

Begin to claim it by faith. When you get up every morning, anticipate the favor of God going before you. Anticipate the favor of God surrounding you. Expect God to give you favor with men—even with the ungodly. If you do, God will open doors for you that neither man nor the devil can shut.

Don't Shoot!

Chapter 12

*"The heart of the righteous
studieth to answer: but the
mouth of the wicked poureth
out evil things."*
— PROVERBS 15:28

Keith Moore

In Psalm 64:3, David compared words to
arrows. The wicked, he said, *"sharpen their
tongues like swords and aim their words like
deadly arrows"* (NIV).

I was reminded of this comparison some
years ago when I was given a compound bow
and a set of razor-tipped arrows. Because of
its power and the sharpness of the arrows,
this bow is a lethal weapon. Consequently, I
have to be careful how I use it.

As long as I have the bowstring in my
hand, I'm in control of the arrow. But the
moment I release the string, it's no longer
in my control. The arrow will simply go
where it was pointed. I cannot get it back
or slow it down. Once I've loosed it, it's on
its way to a target.

And that's exactly how words are. As long as words are in your mind and in your heart, as long as you haven't spoken them, you've got your hand on the bowstring. You're still in control. You can let the bow back down and not shoot at all. But if you let go of the string—speak the words—the arrow flies. There's no way you can recall words once they're spoken.

And if your words are *"deadly arrows,"* they may do unintended harm.

Suppose I carry my bow to work some morning when I'm angry and just start shooting arrows in every direction. What happens? When I cool off and look, I see people lying all around with arrows sticking out of them.

Of course, I can run over to the nearest victim and apologize. "Oh, man, I'm sorry. I was upset about something. I didn't mean to shoot you. I wasn't even thinking about you. I wasn't aiming for you. I was just shooting. I'm sorry!"

But the trouble is—you're still shot! I can pull the arrow out and pour oil and wine on the wound, but no matter how much I apologize, I can't unsay the words that wounded you. You're still shot, and I have some idle words to give account of to God (Matthew 12:36).

We can avoid disasters like this by following the principles in God's Word. Proverbs 15:28 says, *"The heart of the righteous studieth to answer: but the mouth of the wicked poureth out evil things."* And James 1:19 tells us to be *"slow to speak."*

So, the next time you're tempted to "shoot off your mouth," stop and consider whether your words may become *"deadly arrows."* Study the effect of your words before you speak, and then you won't have to apologize for them later.

Chapter 13

Envy—The Devil's Personal Poison

Gloria Copeland

"The night is far spent, the day is at hand: let us therefore cast off the works of darkness, and let us put on the armour of light. Let us walk honestly, as in the day; not in rioting and drunkenness, not in chambering and wantonness, not in strife and envying. But put ye on the Lord Jesus Christ, and make not provision for the flesh, to fulfil the lusts thereof."

— ROMANS 13:12-14

Envy: A feeling of discontent and ill will because of another's advantages, possessions or success.

It's an experience we've all had at one time or another. It is so common, in fact, most people think it is no big deal. They see it as just a harmless, human emotion. But they are gravely mistaken.

As innocent as it may sometimes seem, envy is actually the devil's own poison, designed to turn love into hate and immobilize the force of faith in your life. If you want to see how deadly envy can be, just take a look through the Scriptures. Find out where it comes from and—more alarming than that—where it is headed. Once you do, you'll want to rid yourself of it once and for all.

"Well, Gloria, that shouldn't be too difficult for me," you may say. "I don't really think I'm envious of anyone."

That may be true. But let me encourage you to search your heart carefully just to be sure, because many times we aren't even conscious of envy. We may feel it stirring within us, but we fail to identify it because we assume such feelings are "only natural."

Actually, "natural" is precisely what envy is. It's part of what the Bible calls the "natural" or "carnal" mind." It's a mind programmed by the devil to be in direct opposition to God.

Another biblical term for it is "the flesh." Envy is listed as *"works of the flesh"* in Galatians 5, and it's put alongside some other very serious sins including: *"Adultery, fornication, uncleanness, lasciviousness, Idolatry, witchcraft, hatred, variance, emulations, wrath, strife, seditions, heresies, Envyings, murders, drunkenness, revellings, and such"* (verses 19-21).

That's not exactly a pretty list, is it?

Most believers would never purposely engage in any of those fleshly activities. How then does envy get into our lives?

It sneaks in without announcing itself. It slips in unnoticed.

Suppose you go to church, for instance, and you see Brother Smith with a new car. Suddenly a thought comes to your mind: *Why does he have a new car? He didn't even need it. I'm the one who needs a new car.*

Or suppose you see Sister Jones in a beautiful new dress. As you sit down next to her, you notice how dowdy your dress is compared to hers. Suddenly you feel like someone's ugly stepsister.

You may not think much more about it—consciously. But later, you notice you're a little irritated or depressed. You can't quite put your finger on why you feel that way. After all, you were having a good day until a little while ago. What happened?

I'll tell you what happened. Envy crept in and poisoned you with a feeling of ill will and discontent because of another's success or advantages. Envy made a move on you.

Pulling the Plug on Your Faith

Notice I said it made a move on you, not in you. That's an important distinction.

You see, if you're a born-again believer, envy is not a part of your spiritual nature. It's something the devil tries to pressure you into receiving. He dangles it in front of you like bait on a hook, hoping you'll take a bite.

Why? Because he wants to defeat you! He wants to keep you sick, broke, sad and perpetually trapped beneath your circumstances. And to do that, he must somehow stop you from living by faith.

Since he can't very well just come barreling in the front door and steal the faith right out of your heart, he slips in the back way. He uses envy and strife to interrupt the flow of love in your life.

The minute love is disrupted, your faith stops working too, because faith works by love (Galatians 5:6).

Many Christians don't understand that principle, so they struggle along, quarreling and fussing with one another—and all the while wonder why their faith isn't producing results. They don't realize that if you want to walk in the power and blessing of God, you cannot allow envy or strife into your life. Period.

James 3:16 shows us why that's true. It says, *"Where envying and strife is, there is confusion and every evil work."* In other words, envy and strife give the devil an open door into your life.

What kinds of "evil work" will the devil bring through that open door? Everything from depression to murder. Yes, murder! That was envy's first recorded act. It was responsible for the first human bloodshed.

You can read about it in Genesis 4. There, the Bible tells us:

> In course of time Cain brought to the Lord an offering of the fruit of the ground. And Able brought of the first-born of his flock and of the fat portions. And the Lord had respect and regard for Abel and for his offering. But for Cain and his offering He had no respect or regard. So Cain was exceedingly angry and indignant, and he looked sad and depressed. And the Lord said to Cain, Why are you angry? And why do you look sad and dejected? If you do well, will you not be accepted? And if you do not do well, sin crouches at your door; its desire is for you, and you must master it (verses 3-7, AMP).

What was Cain feeling? He was feeling envy because his brother had the Lord's approval and he didn't.

Now, notice the Lord didn't say, "Oh, Cain, don't worry about that. After all, those feelings are only natural. You're just experiencing a little sibling rivalry."

No, He said, "Cain, sin is crouching at your door."

We all need to heed those words. We need to realize that envy is sin. It's the opposite of love. It is of the devil and if we let it stay in our lives, very soon we'll be yielding to the evil spirit that governs it. That's what Cain did, and as a result he *"rose up against Abel his brother, and killed him"* (verse 8, AMP).

That wasn't an isolated incident either. You can follow the deadly tracks of envy all the way through the Bible.

Psalm 106, for example, says Dathan envied Moses and Aaron. You know what happened to him, don't you? He was swallowed up by the earth.

Envy sparked Jacob's sons to sell Joseph into slavery just to get rid of him. But instead of getting better, their lives grew worse. Finally, they had to go to another country to get enough food to keep their families from starving to death.

In the New Testament, the Pharisees' attitude toward Jesus was poisoned by envy. Ultimately, we know it drove them to kill Him, for Matthew 27:18 says, *"It was because of envy that they had handed Him over to [Pilate]"* (AMP).

From Genesis to Revelation, you can see envy doing its sinister work, trying to stop the plan of God.

Even When You're Right... You're Wrong

No wonder the Apostle John warns us so strongly against it, saying:

This is the message...which you have heard from the first, that we should love one another, [And] not be like Cain who [took his nature and got his motivation] from the evil one and slew his brother...He who does not love abides—remains, is held and kept continually—in [spiritual] death. Any one who... hates his brother [in Christ] is [at heart] a murderer, and you know

**that no murderer has eternal life
abiding (persevering) within him
(1 John 3:11-12, 14-15, AMP).**

Clearly, envy is serious business. We need
to rid ourselves of it completely and start
loving each other. We need to stop striving
with each other and *"lay [our] lives down
for [those who are our] brothers [in Him]"*
(verse 16).

That's what real love is, you know—
laying down your life for someone else. And
in a very real sense, you are laying down
your life when you refuse to envy, because
envy tries to get you to fight for your own
rights. It pushes you to look out for your
own welfare and to be hostile because
someone else is more successful in life than
you are.

Ironically, however, what envy actually
does is stop your success. It keeps you from
rising to the level of those you are envying.
Why? Because, as I said before, it stops
your faith. It takes you outside the realm of
love, and 1 Corinthians 13:8 says love never
fails. Therefore, envy becomes a trap that
secures your failure!

The truth is, all strife works that way—whether it's caused by envy or by something else. All strife is sin!

That means even when you are on the "right" side of an argument, if you're in strife, you're wrong. When you're offended and angry with your husband or wife, your children or anyone else, you're wrong. You've opened the door to the devil and you'd better do something quickly.

What should you do?

Shut the door! Stubbornly resist those fleshly pressures and temptations of the devil. Treat strife just as you'd treat a rattlesnake or any other deadly invader. Refuse to let it in!

If you're a preacher of the gospel, for instance, and there's a new pastor in town who is getting more results than you are, don't be naive enough to fall into the trap that envy is setting. Trick the devil! Turn the tables on him! Start praising God for the success of the new pastor. Do what you can to help him.

In other words, start walking in love and laying down selfishness. If you'll do that, you'll keep the door open for the blessings of God.

You Can Do It!

That's important because in this dangerous day, we need God's blessings more than ever. We need His power. We need to be walking in our full inheritance as believers because this age is about to be brought to a close. As the Apostle Paul says:

> The night is far gone [and] the day is almost here. Let us then drop (fling away) the works and deeds of darkness and put on the [full] armor of light. Let us live and conduct ourselves honorably and becomingly as in the [open light of] day; not in reveling (carousing) and drunkenness, not in immorality and debauchery...not in quarreling and jealousy. But clothe yourself with the Lord Jesus Christ, the Messiah, and make no provision

167

for [indulging] the flesh (Romans 13:12-14, AMP).

The hour is late! It's time for us to wake up. It's time we quit allowing the devil to darken our homes, our businesses, our churches and our individual lives with strife and envy. It's time we quit letting him pull the plug on our faith power. It's time we started living in the light.

You may be thinking, *That's easier said than done!*

I know. But you can do it.

How? Learn to watch over yourself. Pay attention to your state of mind. When you find yourself depressed or downcast, don't just ignore those feelings. Think back. Ask yourself, "What started this downturn?"

You may realize that a particular situation sparked feelings of aggravation, jealousy or strife within you. If so, look at that situation through the eyes of God and then talk to it (see Mark 11:23).

Say, "That situation has no power over me. I refuse to allow it to bring envy and strife into my life. I yield to the forces of love and joy within me. And, Lord, I praise You for Brother Smith's new car. I thank You that Sister Jones has those nice clothes!"

Then just start praising the Lord. Sing a song. Put on a tape that will lift you up, and force yourself to sing along. Before long, the love of God will be bubbling up out of your heart again and you'll be singing in genuine joy.

I know you will, because I've done it!

That's right. These are not just good ideas I'm giving you. They are principles from the Word of God that Ken and I have lived by for more than 30 years now. They are principles that have literally changed our lives.

They'll change your life, too. In fact, I believe any husband and wife who will live the life of love described in 1 Corinthians 13:4-8 can have a wonderful life together. Even if they start off at zero with no love between them at all, they can end up with a successful marriage because love never fails!

"But, Gloria, if love never fails, why do so many Christian marriages—marriages that were once based on the love of God—end up on the rocks?" you ask.

It happens because strife and envy are allowed to cut that love short. As a result, those Christian lives and marriages are drained of God's power. They become carnal, and there is confusion and every evil work.

First Corinthians 3:3 puts it this way: *"For as long as [there are] envying and jealousy...among you, are you not unspiritual and of the flesh, behaving yourselves...like mere (unchanged) men?"* (AMP).

The moment we let envy and strife in the door, we begin to live like people out there in the world. We become like the natural, unsaved men in this scripture—fearful, powerless and defeated—instead of like supernatural, born-again, Spirit-filled people of God.

I agree with Paul. The hour is too late for us to live like that. The coming of Jesus is near at hand. And when He comes, we don't want Him to find us spiritually sick and weak, living lives that have been poisoned by envy and strife.

We want Him to find us standing tall in the spirit—full of love, faith and power—walking in the victory Jesus bought for us.

We want Him to find us living in the light!

Chapter 14

Destined to Lead: How to Become the Leader God Designed You to Be

Mac Hammond

"He that entereth in by the door is the shepherd of the sheep. To him the porter openeth; and the sheep hear his voice: and he calleth his own sheep by name, and leadeth them out."
— JOHN 10:2-3

Follow the leader. It's a game so simple even the smallest child can play it. All you need is one person bold enough to march out front and a few others cooperative enough to follow behind. Right?

Not really. But, sadly enough, that's the mistaken idea many believers have today. It's an idea that has hindered the growth of Christian businesses, ministries and the Church at large. And it's time we began to correct it.

It's time we became the leaders God intended us to be.

At first glance, it might appear that we already have more than enough leaders. But the truth is, what we actually have is a surplus of people who think they're leaders but they aren't. We've all seen them (and at one time or another could probably be numbered among them)—self-proclaimed leaders who are walking along with no one following them.

Pardon me for stating the obvious, but the very word *leader* implies that a person has the ability to obtain followers. It refers to someone who has been able to exercise enough influence over other people to convince them to go in a particular direction. The person who is marching ahead with no one behind him isn't leading—he's just taking a walk!

Another basic quality of leadership is the ability to organize those who are following in order to achieve a stated purpose or desired result. In other words, a real leader can mobilize people, meet goals and make things happen.

More Than a Title

Now, in the light of that information, I'd like you to ask yourself, "Am I a leader?"

If you're born again, you're called to be one. That's right. At the most basic level, every member of the Body of Christ is divinely destined to lead others into the kingdom of God. We're all called to influence people for Jesus.

Once we're faithful in that area, God will promote us to other positions of leadership. Generally, that's where the problems begin. That's because many people think once they've been given positions or titles of authority that the positions themselves make them leaders. Nothing could be further from the truth.

It doesn't matter what the sign says on your office door, how skilled you are technically, how many college degrees you have, how much product knowledge or marketing savvy you've accumulated, you are a true leader only when you are following the example of the greatest leader of all time, the Lord Jesus Christ.

In John 10, Jesus compares His leadership style to that of a shepherd, saying:

He that entereth in by the door is the shepherd of the sheep. To him the porter openeth; and the sheep hear his voice: and he calleth his own sheep by name, and leadeth them out. And when he putteth forth his own sheep, he goeth before them, and the sheep follow him: for they know his voice. And a stranger will they not follow, but will flee from him: for they know not the voice of strangers...I am the good shepherd, and know my sheep, and am known of mine. As the Father knoweth me, even so know I the Father: and I lay down my life for the sheep (verses 2-5, 14-15).

Getting to Know You

The first thing I'd like you to notice about that passage of Scripture is the fact that Jesus said the sheep follow Him because they know Him and He knows them. What does it mean to know someone? It means to have a relationship with him.

Therefore, according to Jesus, leadership is first and foremost a relational skill.

The secular world stumbled on that fact themselves a few years ago. They thought they had really come up with a brilliant idea. (It's always funny to me to see the world discover some new principle that's been in the Bible for 2,000 years.) A recent Stanford University study of several thousand executives in the corporate and entrepreneurial world revealed that 85 percent of the success of those business people could be attributed not to their product knowledge, but to their skill in cultivating relationships with people.

That's a scriptural truth, and it works in ministries and churches just as surely as it works in the business world. No matter what your arena of authority, you cannot lead effectively unless you know the people you're leading and they know you!

Some might say that's impossible. After all, if an organization grows to hundreds or even thousands of people, the head of that organization could never get to know every one of them. So, what's the solution?

Again, the corporate world has discovered what Jesus knew long ago, one person can personally administrate no more than 12 people. So, in larger organizations, the top leader must cultivate a leadership group of 12 (or fewer) under him. Those leaders are, in turn, responsible for a similar group under them, and so on.

Thus, no matter what level of leadership you hold, it's those people who are directly accountable to you that you, as a leader, need to know. That means you must spend time with them, not just giving them instructions, but talking to them, learning to understand their priorities and value systems, what motivates them and what doesn't, their strengths and their weaknesses.

As their leader, you need to know how they respond to various circumstances. You need to discover the areas in which they need to be supported and find out what skills they have that can be best utilized to achieve the goal that you desire.

Just as importantly, they need to know you—not just the "strong leader" facade you've created to impress people, but the real, genuine you!

That means you must be open and honest with those you're leading. You must make sure you don't have any hidden motives they can't see, that you don't say one thing when you mean another or profess loyalty to them as individuals, but then act like your only concern is getting the job done.

In 1 Thessalonians 5, the Apostle Paul actually gives Christians a scriptural mandate to *"know them which labour among you, and are over you in the Lord, and admonish you; And to esteem them very highly in love for their work's sake"* (verses 12-13). Notice the connection there between knowing and esteem. Esteem isn't something that just happens. It comes when people become familiar with the person they're serving and begin to trust him.

Be the Same Yesterday, Today And...

Of course, if those you're leading get to know you and discover you're not worthy of their trust, you'll have a problem. So it's vitally important that as leaders we conduct ourselves in a trustworthy manner.

That means, for instance, being forthright with people. If someone does something that you don't like or that is contrary to your instructions, don't criticize him behind his back. Don't just block his raise or send him a notice of termination. Communicate frankly and directly.

Go to him personally and say, "Hey, you made a mistake. I know you didn't have a wrong motive. So let's talk about it and see if we can prevent that kind of thing from happening again."

You can also elevate the trust factor by being consistent. The reason we can trust Jesus so implicitly is that He is *"the same yesterday, and today, and for ever"* (Hebrews 13:8). You can't trust someone who is not consistent in his response to you.

The worst person in the world to work for is someone who is high one day and low the next in his relationships with people. It's the employer who is so erratic that his employees can't ever predict with any regularity how he is going to respond to them. They're reluctant to talk to their boss about anything, because they don't know if he is going to bite their heads off or be polite.

Don't be that way. Give the people you lead reason to trust you by responding to them consistently and in love, day after day. Then step out and lead as Jesus did, not by barking orders from behind, but by walking before them and showing the way.

The Leadership Anointing

Look back at John 10 and you'll see what I mean. There Jesus says the shepherd *"goeth before them, and the sheep follow him"* (verse 4). He was showing us that an effective leader always steps forward and acts as an example for his followers.

In my church, for instance, we set a goal each year and specify the number of confirmed salvations we want to see by the end of the year. One year our goal was 35,000, and we exceeded that number considerably. But we wouldn't have if I had just told the congregation, "Now, you all go out and witness to people," then left it at that. No, the congregation had to see that goal incorporated into the lives of the pastoral staff. They had to see their leaders modeling those values and giving them an example to follow.

Here's a fact that will stand you in good stead as long as God entrusts you with leadership responsibility: If you're not seeing the character qualities, work ethics or values that you want to see in the people who work for you, it's because they're not seeing them in you.

As a whole, the people you lead will be a mirror reflection of you. (I'm not talking about the folks who have only been with you for a few months or about isolated problem individuals. I'm referring to the overall trends you see recurring among those who have served you for a significant length of time.) You might assume that reflection is simply a natural result of their watching and learning from you. There is, however, much more to it than that.

The Bible clearly teaches that God equips those He calls. So if He elevates you to a position of responsibility, you can be assured He will also anoint you to impart direction to the people under your care. That's a supernatural principle, and you can see it operating at every level of leadership.

Take parenting, for example. God has equipped us as parents to supernaturally influence the direction of our children. And, much to our dismay, we usually find that the weaknesses we see in our children mirror the weaknesses in our own characters or personalities.

That's why in the majority of cases, alcoholic parents produce alcoholic children. You'd think such children would be driven away from alcohol after seeing the devastation it brought forth in their parents' lives. But because of the supernatural anointing of leadership, they most often follow in the footsteps of their mother and father despite their hatred of the alcoholic lifestyle.

Once you, as a leader, understand that principle, you'll realize that if you want to correct a fault or weakness in the group you've been appointed and anointed to lead, that correction will have to begin with you.

Now, with all that said, let me ask you again: Are you a leader?

You're called to be. And heaven knows the Body of Christ is in desperate need of more people who will answer that call. People who know that leadership isn't child's play. People who are willing to take the time to know, be known by, and earn the trust of, those who follow them.

Now more than ever, God is searching for people who will walk in the steps of the Good Shepherd. He is wanting believers in every realm of life—in homes, in businesses, in churches and in communities—who will truly lead His sheep.

You can be one of them. Will you?

Dressed for Success

Chapter 15

*"Put on the full armor of God,
that you may be able to stand firm
against the schemes of the devil."*
— EPHESIANS 6:11, NAS

Jerry Savelle

Have you ever felt that you've been resisting the devil firm in your faith so long you can't resist any longer? Having done all to stand, you've stood, but you think you can't stand anymore? Have you found yourself praying, "God, I don't care if I overcome. Just let me survive. And if I ever get out of this, I promise, I'll never use my faith again"?

I have. In fact, I've learned we're most vulnerable right after a victory. We've had fiery darts coming our way for quite some time, and some of them have penetrated. After a while, we just want to get our armor off because that shield of faith has become so heavy with all those darts in it. That helmet of salvation has started leaning to one side. The belt of truth has begun to slide a little. We've gotten some gook on our gospel shoes, and we just keep losing ground. The breastplate of righteousness won't stay on.

When we finally win a battle, we want to take a spiritual vacation. We want to take our armor off, pile it in the corner and hope to God we don't have to use our faith for at least another six months. And that's when the devil attacks.

Right Where You Want Him

I remember one time when I had stood and done everything to stand, but I felt as if I couldn't stand anymore. I felt as if my helmet was falling off. My shield of faith didn't have room for another dart. My breastplate was just barely on. I was standing there asking God, "What do I do next?"

And He said, *Rejoice.*

I said, "Say what?"

He said, *Rejoice. You've got the devil right where you want him.*

I said, "Is anybody else up there? I'd like a second opinion on this."

Then I said, "God, have You looked at me lately? I'm just barely dressed here. The armor's falling off. There's not room for another dart in my shield of faith. My sword's limp."

He said, *Rejoice. You've got the devil right where you want him.*

I said, "God, You're not listening to me. I don't know if I can stand anymore. How can I rejoice?"

He said, *Son, when you're under the greatest pressure to quit, it's an indication that the enemy has fired his best shot, and if that shot doesn't get you, he's finished. You may be shaky and feel as if your armor's falling off—but take a look. You are still standing.*

Right now, if you're under the greatest pressure you've ever been under, you've got the devil right where you want him. And I want to give you the successful strategy that God gave me for winning. I want to show you how to dress for battle and how to take an aggressive stand against the enemy. I want to show you how to enlist in God's army and how to conduct yourself in battle so that you will not only overcome the enemy, but will take back all that has been stolen from you.

Full Battle Dress

In order to take an aggressive stand of faith, you must get properly dressed and equipped for battle.

> **Put on the full armor of God, that you may be able to stand firm against the schemes of the devil... Stand firm therefore, having girded your loins with truth, and having put on the breastplate of righteousness, and having shod your feet with the preparation of the gospel of peace; in addition to all, taking up the shield of faith with which you will be able to extinguish all the flaming missiles of the evil one. And take the helmet of salvation, and the sword of the Spirit, which**

is the word of God (Ephesians 6:11, 14-17, NAS).

Stand Firm

The next step in your strategy, after you have put on your armor, is to determine that you will not compromise on your stand of faith. Tell the devil: "If it's a fight you want, a fight you'll get, but when the dust settles, God and I will still be standing."

Stand firm! Take the shield of faith and extinguish all the flaming missiles the enemy fires at you! Notice that the *New American Standard* version says *"flaming missiles"* instead of *"fiery darts" (King James Version)*. It seems as if the devil quit throwing fiery darts years ago. Fiery darts were bad enough. Now it's missiles.

But God says, *Rejoice*. Satan has fired his best shot, and if you refuse to quit, refuse to give up, if you'll stand firm, there's not a thing he can do to win over you. He may go from darts to missiles, but, thank God, the Holy Ghost will supply you with power to overcome.

But you have to stand firm. Let me remind you the Bible says that the weapons of our warfare are mighty through God (2 Corinthians 10:4). You and I have been well equipped for battle. God has not left us helpless. God has not left us without proper weapons of warfare, and He has chosen us to be soldiers in His army. All we have to do is enlist!

You're in the Army Now!

Sometimes I feel sorry for God. He's Commander in Chief of an army, but have you looked at this army lately? Half of God's army doesn't even know who the enemy is. How would you like to be commander in chief when half your troops have their weapons pointed toward headquarters? "God, why'd You do this to me? Oh, God, You made me sick. Oh, God, You wrecked my car. Oh, God, why'd You do this to me?"

Or how would you like to be commander in chief of an army that refuses to dress properly? God tells His troops to put on His whole armor, and some of them will wear only a helmet: "Oh, we believe in salvation." Don't you know they're a sight in the spirit realm, confronting the enemy with nothing on but a helmet?

Another group says, "There's none righteous, no not one." No breastplate. "We don't believe in that faith stuff." No shield. And God has to put up with this.

I remember when I was inducted into the armed forces in 1967 at Fort Dix, New Jersey, with some other young men. Waiting for us was a man dressed like Smokey Bear who lined us up, got right in our faces and walked up and down the line screaming some of the most vulgar things I'd ever heard.

Now this was during the hippie movement, and right next to me in line was a hippie. I'll never forget him. He had on bright, green-and-white striped, bell-bottom, hip-hugger pants with flowers sewn all over them. He had hair down to the middle of his back. He was so stoned he didn't know he was there yet. The sergeant put his nose right up next to the hippie's nose and screamed, "I'm going to make a soldier out of you whether you like it or not." The hippie kind of woke up about that time and said, "Peace, brother, peace."

Farther down the line was a boy from Mississippi in bib overalls and a straw hat. Next to him was a man in a three-piece suit who looked like a banker.

And there I was. I had come right out of the paint and body shop. I had short hair and had on black slacks and a yellow, pull-over knit shirt.

I looked down that line at all those boys they were going to make soldiers of, and I thought, *Dear God, this country is in serious trouble. We've got a war going on and look what we've got to work with here.*

But you know what? In eight weeks, I didn't look, talk, act or dress like a civilian. By the time I graduated from boot camp, I'd become a soldier and was proud to be a soldier.

Well, when I first came into the army of God, I looked down the line, and thought, *Dear God, we are in serious trouble. God thinks He'll win the world with this.* But

God is not moved by what He sees. God really believes this army will put death under its feet and conquer Satan in his fortresses. And, praise God, we are going to do it!

No Turning Back

But we won't do it unless we learn proper conduct on the battlefield. We can't be like the sons of Ephraim in Psalm 78. They were equipped with weapons and were skilled warriors. They had won battles before. But verse 9 says, *"Yet they turned back in the day of battle"* (AMP).

That's the story of many Christians today. They turn back in the day of battle. There are some Christians who never really engage in battle. They let the devil talk them into defeat before they ever take a stand.

In the heat of battle, under pressure, they drop their weapons and flee. Negative reports. Two or three upsetting phone calls. Three bills in the mail. And they want to give up.

Don't Panic

Why do they want to give up? Because of fear. Fear is the first thing you have to deal with in battle. In Deuteronomy 20 God tells us how we are to deal with fear on the battlefield: *"When you go out to battle against your enemies and see horses and chariots and people more numerous than you, do not be afraid of them...or panic...for the Lord your God...goes with you, to fight for you"* (verses 1, 3-4, NAS).

God says, "Don't panic." Why? Because when you panic, you forget everything you've learned. I don't care how many meetings you've attended or how many tapes you've listened to, when you panic, you forget everything. Then you can't resist the devil with what you've learned. Don't panic, because *"the Lord your God...goes with you, to fight for you"* (Deuteronomy 20:4, NAS).

Do as David did when he came home to find his entire village burned to the ground, and his wives and the families of his men taken captive. The Bible says he was *"greatly distressed,"* but David *"encouraged himself in the Lord his God"* (1 Samuel 30:6). How? By remembering his covenant. *"A thousand shall fall at [my] side, and ten thousand at [my] right hand..."* (Psalm 91:7). *"The Lord is my shepherd..."* (Psalm 23:1). *"The Lord is...my strength...and my high tower"* (Psalm 18:2).

As he encouraged himself, the strength of God began to flow into him again. Instead of accepting defeat, he asked God, *"Shall I pursue after this troop?"* And God said, *"Pursue... overtake...recover all"* (1 Samuel 30:8).

My friends, these are still God's marching orders to us today. No matter how many darts are sticking in your armor, no matter how greatly distressed you are, get up and encourage yourself in the Lord. You are dressed for success in battle. Now pursue, overtake and recover all.

Walking on Water—
The Secret to
Fulfilling Your Call

Chapter 16

*Gloria
Copeland*

*"This one thing I do, forgetting
those things which are behind, and
reaching forth unto those things
which are before, I press toward
the mark for the prize of the high
calling of God in Christ Jesus."*
— PHILIPPIANS 3:13-14

How many of you feel God has called
you to do something that is absolutely
impossible? That was the question I asked
a group of ministers one time. The number
of hands raised in response was great.
Almost every one of them felt God had called
them to do something they didn't have the
ability to do.

Chances are, if you've been seeking God
and asking Him to show you His plan for
your life, you've run into the very same
thing. Whether you are called to the fivefold
ministry or to serve in some other capacity

in the Body of Christ, the vision God has given you is most likely something completely out of reach—something bigger than you ever dreamed you could do.

If that's the case, I want to encourage you today. I want to share something God told me years ago that took a great deal of pressure off me in the area of ministry. It was this:

Everything God calls us to do is impossible to men.

Now, doesn't that make you feel better? It did me. When God said that to me, I suddenly realized He didn't expect me to know how to do His work. He didn't expect me to have the natural ability or strength to accomplish it.

It lifted the pressure off me to realize that what I have to do in God is impossible anyway. If He doesn't do it through me, it's not going to get done.

Just think about it. You can't lay hands on the sick and have them recover without the Anointing of God on you. You can't cast out devils without the Spirit of God moving through you. You can't even speak in tongues unless the Spirit gives you utterance.

Everything we're called to do in God is impossible with men. Once I realized that, it took the pressure off me—and put it on God. I no longer looked to my ability, or lack of it, but to God's ability.

When God gives us an assignment, He's not depending on us to use our own intelligence and power to complete that assignment. In fact, the Bible says He actually chooses us considering our lack of intelligence and power. First Corinthians 1:26-29 says:

> For ye see your calling, brethren, how that not many wise men after the flesh, not many mighty, not many noble, are called: But God hath chosen the foolish things of the world to confound the wise; and God hath chosen the weak things of the world to confound the things which are mighty; And base things of the world, and things which are despised, hath God chosen, yea, and things which are not, to bring

to nought things that are: That no flesh should glory in his presence.

God knew you weren't smart enough or strong enough to do His work when He called you. That's why He called you. He knew you would have to depend on Him. And, believe me, He knows exactly how to get the job done.

I remember, years ago, when we were living in Tulsa, Oklahoma, and Ken was a student at Oral Roberts University. One day he went down to the riverbed behind our house to pray, and God spoke to him about ministering to nations.

Now, at that time in our lives we could hardly afford to get across town. But God said, *You are going to minister to nations.*

That was so impossible. Nobody even knew who we were. We didn't have any money. Just getting to Texas to visit Ken's parents was a big deal—and God was talking about nations!

We've been in the ministry more than 30 years now. In January of 1990, God spoke to Kenneth again and told him,

You're just now in position to do the main work I've called you to do.

Now things are happening in the nations. Nations are opening up to us. We're going on television in the Baltic Sea States. We're also on the air in the Scandinavian countries. Doors are opening everywhere.

We're not trying to do it. God is taking care of it all. It thrills me to think of that!

He didn't expect Ken and me to know how to reach nations. He knew we didn't have an extra $15 to get from one state to the other when He told us to go into all the world and preach the gospel. But God is not broke. He had the money. He knew where it was.

He has paid every bill all these years. We didn't need it in the bank. He had it!

God doesn't expect us to have the resources or the know-how to do His work. Do you know what He expects from us? He just expects us to take the next step.

All He wants is for us to spend time with Him, to pray and find out what He wants us to do next. He'll always reveal to you the next step to take. He may not show you any more than that, but you can be sure He will tell you the next step.

I like to compare it to walking on water as Peter did in Matthew 14. You know, walking on water is an impossible thing to do! Peter had absolutely no ability to do it. Yet, Jesus said to him simply, *"Come,"* and Peter jumped over the side of that boat and started walking. When he did, sure enough, the power of the word of Jesus took hold of him and held him up.

But then something happened. Verse 30 says, *"But when he [Peter] saw the wind boisterous, he was afraid; and beginning to sink, he cried, saying, Lord, save me."*

Take note of that. Peter was walking on the water just fine until he took his eyes away from Jesus and started looking somewhere else. He started looking at the size of the waves. He started looking at the circumstance. And he started to sink.

Every failure you've ever had in your Christian life has come exactly that way. It has come because you've quit looking at

Who called you and quit trusting in His Word and started focusing on the problems around you instead.

That is what stops the people of God. It's not the lack of God's power. It's not that He is unwilling to move and do supernatural things on our behalf. What stops us is our taking our attention off Jesus and putting it on our circumstances.

"Oh, but Gloria," you may say, "you don't understand how really bad my circumstances are."

It doesn't matter how bad they are! For years the Apostle Paul was faced with the worst circumstances you could imagine. He was imprisoned, beaten, shipwrecked and abused in almost every way imaginable for preaching the gospel. But those things didn't stop him. At the end of his life he was able to say, *"I have finished my course."*

Paul fulfilled an impossible call in the midst of impossible circumstances. How did he do it? He tells us in Philippians 3:13-14: *"This one thing I do, forgetting those things which are behind, and reaching forth unto those things which are before, I press toward the mark for the prize of the high calling of God in Christ Jesus."*

Paul had his eye on the prize. He was looking ahead. He wasn't looking at today. He wasn't looking at his problems. Paul focused his eyes on Jesus and on the goal Jesus had set before him. That focus carried him through in triumph.

The same thing is true for us today which was true for Paul. If we're going to do the impossible, there's only one way to do it— by keeping our eyes on Jesus, the One Who is Lord over this universe.

One thing you need to be aware of, however, is this: It's not always the problems of this life that distract us. Sometimes it's the pleasures. Sometimes we just allow the natural things of living to draw us off course. If you're going to run your race effectively, you'll have to lay aside some things.

Hebrews 12:1 says, *"Wherefore seeing we also are compassed about with so great a cloud of witnesses, let us lay aside every weight, and the sin which doth so easily beset us, and let us run with patience the race that is set before us."*

Weights and sin are not the same thing. Most of us are willing to lay aside sin. But we're reluctant to let go of those "harmless" things that just weigh us down. Things which occupy the time we need to be spending in prayer and the Word, for example. Things that hold us down and keep us in the natural realm instead of allowing us to soar in the spirit.

Weights like that won't just go away by themselves. They have to be purposely laid aside. God won't lay them aside for you. You have to do it.

It's not easy to finish your course. It is easier to fall by the wayside—to let some distracting circumstance or some lying devil talk you into giving up by making you feel inadequate and alone.

If that has happened to you, let me tell you something today. In yourself, you are inadequate. But you're not alone! That makes all the difference.

When God spoke to the faith heroes in the Old Testament—men like Moses and Joshua—He would always say, "Don't be afraid, for I am with you. It doesn't really matter who you are. It is Who is with you that counts!"

God didn't expect Joshua to be able to knock over the walls of Jericho with his own strength. Those walls were going to come down supernaturally. All Joshua had to do was trust God and take the next step. God told Joshua, *"Be strong and of a good courage; be not afraid, neither be thou dismayed: for the Lord thy God is with thee whithersoever thou goest"* (Joshua 1:9).

He's saying the same thing to you today. "Don't be afraid. Be strong. Be courageous, for I am with you!" That's the thing we have to remember. God is in us. He is with us.

If God has given you an impossible assignment, don't worry about it. He knows exactly how to complete it. And He intends to complete it through you.

It's the Anointed One in you Who is going to do the work. It's the Spirit of God

Who will bring those impossible things to pass. All you have to do is take the next step.

Of course, you will have to do some things to find out what that next step is. You'll have to spend time in the Word, time praying in the spirit, time listening for and expecting to hear His direction.

But don't expect Him to give you 10 steps at one time. He rarely does. He just tells you what you can do today.

The secret is to be trusting and simple, to come as a little child before the Lord and hear from Him every day. Don't try to figure out all the things you need to do and how to do them. Just listen day by day, take one step at a time, and you will come to the place where God wants you to be. You will finish your race.

In the meantime, don't be weighed down with the need to get everything done right now. Don't struggle along, trying to hurry up the process. Learn to obey and, day by day, let God get it done on His schedule.

Kenneth Hagin prophesied not too long ago that days of preparation are never wasted days. So if you feel as if you haven't arrived yet, relax. You haven't arrived yet! But if you're out there walking on the water with your eyes on Jesus, taking one step at a time, you're well on your way.

Prayer for Salvation and Baptism in the Holy Spirit

Heavenly Father, I come to You in the Name of Jesus. Your Word says, *"Whosoever shall call on the name of the Lord shall be saved"* (Acts 2:21). I am calling on You. I pray and ask Jesus to come into my heart and be Lord over my life according to Romans 10:9-10. *"If thou shalt confess with thy mouth the Lord Jesus, and shalt believe in thine heart that God hath raised him from the dead, thou shalt be saved. For with the heart man believeth unto righteousness; and with the mouth confession is made unto salvation."* I do that now. I confess that Jesus is Lord, and I believe in my heart that God raised Him from the dead.

I am now reborn! I am a Christian—a child of Almighty God! I am saved! You also said in Your Word, *"If ye then, being evil, know how to give good gifts unto your children: HOW MUCH MORE shall your heavenly Father give the Holy Spirit to them that ask him?"* (Luke 11:13). I'm also asking You to fill me with the Holy Spirit. Holy Spirit, rise up within me as I praise God. I fully expect to speak with other tongues as You give me the utterance (Acts 2:4).

Begin to praise God for filling you with the Holy Spirit. Speak those words and syllables you receive—not in your own language, but the language given to you by the Holy Spirit. You have to use your own voice. God will not force you to speak. Worship and praise Him in your heavenly language—in other tongues.

Continue with the blessing God has given you and pray in tongues each day.

You are a born-again, Spirit-filled believer. You'll never be the same!

Find a good Word of God preaching church, and become a part of a church family who will love and care for you as you love and care for them.

We need to be hooked up to each other. It increases our strength in God. It's God's plan for us.

Books Available
From
Kenneth Copeland Ministries

by Kenneth Copeland

* A Ceremony of Marriage
  A Matter of Choice
  Covenant of Blood
  Faith and Patience—The Power Twins
* Freedom From Fear
  Giving and Receiving
  Honor—Walking in Honesty, Truth and Integrity
  How to Conquer Strife
  How to Discipline Your Flesh
  How to Receive Communion
  Living at the End of Time—
      A Time of Supernatural Increase
  Love Never Fails
  Managing God's Mutual Funds
* Now Are We in Christ Jesus
* Our Covenant With God
* Prayer—Your Foundation for Success
* Prosperity: The Choice Is Yours
  Rumors of War
* Sensitivity of Heart
* Six Steps to Excellence in Ministry
  Sorrow Not! Winning Over Grief and Sorrow
* The Decision Is Yours
* The Force of Faith
* The Force of Righteousness
  The Image of God in You
  The Laws of Prosperity
* The Mercy of God
  The Miraculous Realm of God's Love
  The Outpouring of the Spirit—The Result of Prayer
* The Power of the Tongue
  The Power to Be Forever Free
  The Troublemaker
* The Winning Attitude

Turn Your Hurts Into Harvests
* Welcome to the Family
* You Are Healed!
Your Right-Standing With God

by Gloria Copeland
* And Jesus Healed Them All
Are You Ready?
Build Your Financial Foundation
Build Yourself an Ark
Fight On!
God's Prescription for Divine Health
God's Success Formula
God's Will for You
God's Will for Your Healing
God's Will Is Prosperity
* God's Will Is the Holy Spirit
* Harvest of Health
Hidden Treasures
Living Contact
Living in Heaven's Blessings Now
* Love—The Secret to Your Success
No Deposit—No Return
Pleasing the Father
Pressing In—It's Worth It All
Shine On!
The Power to Live a New Life
The Unbeatable Spirit of Faith
This Same Jesus
* Walk in the Spirit
Walk With God
Well Worth the Wait

Books Co-Authored by Kenneth and Gloria Copeland
Family Promises
Healing Promises
Prosperity Promises

* From Faith to Faith—A Daily Guide to Victory
From Faith to Faith—A Perpetual Calendar

One Word From God Series
- One Word From God Can Change Your Destiny
- One Word From God Can Change Your Family
- One Word From God Can Change Your Finances
- One Word From God Can Change Your Health

Over the Edge—A Youth Devotional
Over the Edge Xtreme Planner for Students—
    Designed for the School Year

Pursuit of His Presence—A Daily Devotional
Pursuit of His Presence—A Perpetual Calendar

Other Books Published by KCP
The First 30 Years—A Journey of Faith
    The story of the lives of
        Kenneth and Gloria Copeland.
Real People. Real Needs. Real Victories.
    A book of testimonies to encourage your faith.

John G. Lake—His Life, His Sermons,
    His Boldness of Faith
The Holiest of All by Andrew Murray
The New Testament in Modern Speech by
    Richard Francis Weymouth

Products Designed for Today's Children and Youth
Baby Praise Board Book
Noah's Ark Coloring Book
The *Shout!* Super-Activity Book

Commander Kellie and the Superkid Adventure Novels
- #1   The Mysterious Presence
- #2   The Quest for the Second Half
- #3   Escape From Jungle Island
- #4   In Pursuit of the Enemy

SWORD Adventure Book

* Available in Spanish

WE'RE HERE FOR YOU!

Join Kenneth and Gloria Copeland and the *Believer's Voice of Victory* broadcast Monday through Friday and every Sunday. Learn how faith in God's Word can take your life from ordinary to extraordinary.

It's some of the most in-depth teaching you'll ever hear on subjects like faith and healing, deliverance and prosperity, protection and hope. And it's all designed to get you where you want to be—*on top!* The teachings are by some of today's best-known ministers, including Kenneth and Gloria Copeland, Jerry Savelle, Charles Capps, Creflo A. Dollar Jr., Kellie Copeland and Edwin Louis Cole.

Whether it's before breakfast, during lunch or after a long day at the office, plan to make *Believer's Voice of Victory* a daily part of your prayer life. See for yourself how one word from God can change your life forever.

You can catch the *Believer's Voice of Victory* broadcast on the following cable and satellite channels:

Sunday
9-9:30 p.m. ET
Cable*/G5,
Channel 3—TBN

Monday through Friday
7-7:30 p.m. ET
Cable*/G1,
Channel 17—INSP

Monday through Friday
6-6:30 a.m. ET
Cable*/G5,
Channel 7—WGN

Monday through Friday
11-11:30 a.m. ET
Cable*/G5,
Channel 3—TBN

Monday through Friday
6:30-7 a.m. ET
Cable*/G5,
Channel 20—BET

Monday through Friday
10:30-11 a.m. CT
Cable*/Spacenet 3,
Transponder 13 - KMPX

*Check your local listings for more times and stations in your area.

WE'RE HERE FOR YOU!

Believer's Voice of Victory Television Broadcast

Join Kenneth and Gloria Copeland and the *Believer's Voice of Victory* broadcasts Monday through Friday and on Sunday each week, and learn how faith in God's Word can take your life from ordinary to extraordinary. This is some of the best teaching you'll ever hear, designed to get you where you want to be— *on top!*

You can catch the *Believer's Voice of Victory* broadcast on your local, cable or satellite channels.

* Check your local listings for
times and stations in your area.

Believer's Voice of Victory Magazine

Enjoy inspired teaching and encouragement from Kenneth and Gloria Copeland each month in the *Believer's Voice of Victory* magazine. Also included are real-life testimonies of God's miraculous power and divine intervention into the lives of people just like you!

It's more than just a magazine—it's a ministry.

Shout! ...The dynamic magazine just for kids!

Shout! The Voice of Victory for Kids is a Bible-charged, action-packed, bimonthly magazine available FREE to kids everywhere! Featuring *Wichita Slim* and *Commander Kellie and the Superkids, Shout!* is filled with colorful adventure comics, challenging games and puzzles, exciting short stories, solve-it-yourself mysteries and much more!!

Stand up, sign up and get ready to *Shout!*

World Offices
of Kenneth Copeland Ministries

For more information about KCM and a free
catalog, please write the office nearest you:

Kenneth Copeland Ministries
Fort Worth, TX 76192-0001

Kenneth Copeland
Locked Bag 2600
Mansfield Delivery Centre
QUEENSLAND 4122
AUSTRALIA

Kenneth Copeland
Post Office Box 15
BATH
BA1 1GD
ENGLAND U.K.

Kenneth Copeland
Private Bag X 909
FONTAINEBLEAU
2032
REPUBLIC OF SOUTH AFRICA

Kenneth Copeland
Post Office Box 378
Surrey
BRITISH COLUMBIA
V3T 5B6
CANADA

UKRAINE
L'VIV 290000
Post Office Box 84
Kenneth Copeland Ministries
L'VIV 290000
UKRAINE

The Harrison House Vision

Proclaiming the truth and the power
Of the Gospel of Jesus Christ
With excellence;

Challenging Christians to
Live victoriously,
Grow spiritually,
Know God intimately.